Place

Lecce
the Baroque town

Table of content

1. History
    1. A brief history of Lecce - *8*
    2. The historic centre - *10*
        1. Porta San Biagio - *10*
        2. Chiesa Madre di Dio e di San Nicolò - *10*
        3. Chiesa di San Matteo - *11*
        4. Chiesa di San Giuseppe - *12*
        5. Castello Carlo V. - *13*
        6. Piazza Sant'Oronzo - *14*
            1. Colonna di Santo Oronzo - *14*
            2. Anfiteatro Romano - *15*
            3. Palazzo del Sedile - *16*
            4. Chiesa di S. M. delle Grazie - *17*
        7. Chiesa di Santa Irene - *17*
        8. Piazza Duomo - *18*
            1. Campanile - *19*
            2. Duomo - 19
            3. Palazzo Vescovile - *21*
            4. Palazzo del Seminario - *22*
        9. Chiesa di Santa Teresa - *23*
        10. Chiesa di Sant'Anna ed il Conservatorio - *24*
        11. Chiesa di S.G. Battista al Rosario - *25*
        12. Convento dei Domenicani - *26*
        13. Porta Rudiae - *27*
        14. Palazzo Marrese - *28*
        15. Palazzo Palmieri - *28*
        16. Teatro Paisiello - *29*
        17. Chiesa di Santa Maria della Porta - *30*
        18. Porta Napoli - *30*
        19. Obelisco - *31*
        20. Chiesa delle Alcantarine - *31*

21. Chiesa di Santa Maria degli Angeli - *32*
22. Chiesa di S.G. Evangelista - *33*
23. Chiesa di Sant'Angelo - *33*
24. Chiesa Greca - *34*
25. Palazzo Adorno - *35*
26. Convento dei Celestini - *35*
27. Basilica di Santa Croce - *36*
28. Arco di Prato - *37*
29. Chiesa del Gesù - *38*
30. Palazzo Carafa - *38*
31. Chiesa di Santa Chiara - *39*
32. Teatro Romano - *40*
33. Chiesa del Carmine - *40*
34. Chiesa dei S.S. Niccolò e Cataldo - *41*

3. Museums - *42*
   1. Museo Archeologico P. S. Castromediano - *42*
   2. Museo Storico Arch. (MUSA) - *43*
   3. Museo Storio della città di Lecce (MUST) - *43*
   4. Museo Diocesano di Arte Sacra - *44*
   5. Museo Del Teatro Romano - *45*
   6. Mostra Permanente dell'Artigianato Sal. - *45*
   7. Pinacoteca d'Arte Francescana - *46*
   8. Museo Papirologico - *46*
   9. Museo Faggiano - *47*
4. Theatres - *48*
5. Annual events - *49*
   1. Feast of Saint Oronzo - *49*
   2. Open courtyards - *49*
   3. European Film Festival - *50*
   4. Puglia Open Days Winter - *50*

2. The surroundings
   1. Archaeological sites - *51*
      1. Parco Archeologico di Rudiae - *51*
   2. Monasteries - *52*

      1. Abbazia di Santa Maria di Cerrate - *52*

   3. Nature reserves - *53*

      1. Parco Regionale Boschi e Paludi di Rauccio - *53*

      2. Oasi Naturalistica Bacino Costiero Acquatina - *54*

      3. Bacino dell'Idume - *55*

      4. Riserva Naturale San Cataldo - *56*

      5. Riserva Naturale dello Stato Le Cesine - *56*

   4. Beaches - *58*

      1. San Cataldo - 58

      2. Frigole - *58*

      3. Torre Chianca - *59*

      4. Torre Rinalda - *60*

      5. Casalabate - *60*

3. La dolce vita

      1. Local cuisine - *62*

      2. Best restaurants in Lecce - *65*

      3. Bars & café - *68*

      4. Gelaterie & pasticcerie - *70*

4. Sport

      1. Golf - *72*

      2. Swimming - *73*

      3. Riding - *74*

      4. Canoeing - *75*

      5. Skate, surf and windsurf - *76*

5. Shopping

      1. Crafts - *77*

      2. Art workshops - 79

      3. Markets - *80*

      4. Organic shops - *80*

      5. Wine shops - *81*

6. General info

      1. Lecce Wireless City - *83*

      2. Bikesharing - *86*

      3. Taxi service - *86*

    4. Public transports. - *87*
    5. Opening hours - *89*
    6. Practicalities - 90
7. Day trips
    1. Otranto - *98*
    2. Gallipoli - *100*
    3. Ostuni - 102
    4. Alberobello - *104*
    5. Grotte di Castellana - *106*
    6. Castel del Monte - *108*
    7. Martina Franca - *110*
8. Historic centre map - *114*
9. Territory map - *126*
10. Railways map of Puglia - *130*
11. Map of places of interest in Puglia - *136*

Author's note

This guide gives you the information needed to enjoy all that the city has to offer, not only for tourists but also anyone who loves the town.

You will find here information ranging from art to nature, from best restaurants to best bars, pubs, gelaterie and pasticcerie shops. Also advice about sports, shopping and other practicalities.

Please note that restaurants, bars, wine bars etc. listed in this book have been included for their quality, we do not receive any compensation from any of them.

What's inside

Detailed history and art information covering all major monuments of the city of Lecce, such as Baroque churches and palaces, museums and archaeological remains, with references to a map of the historic centre.

All that there is to visit in the territory around the city, from natural parks to beaches and archaeological remains. A map of the area will help you find these places of interest.

Best restaurants, bars, lounge bars, pubs, gelaterie and pasticcerie shops. Also, tips for shopping and sporting activities.

Details of wireless services, transport, bike-sharing, opening hours and other useful information.

Finally, how to reach and visit, within a day, other cities of historic and artistic interest in Puglia.

This book includes four useful maps:

- The historic centre of Lecce;
- The territory around the town;
- The railway network of Puglia, to help anyone who wants to move around by train;
- A complete map of Puglia with places of historical and artistic interest.

1. History

A brief history of Lecce

The origins of Lecce go back to an old Messapian settlement built near the ancient town of Rudiae, home of the Roman writer Ennius. Legend has it was founded around 1200 BC by Malennius, who also introduced Greek culture to the city.

However, it was only under Roman domination that Lecce became an important centre. During this period Emperor Hadrian had the amphitheatre and the theatre built. Later, under Emperor Marcus Aurelius, the city expanded and its economy boomed. At that time it was equipped with a forum and a defensive wall.

After a brief period of Greek domination, Lecce was ruled by the Eastern Roman Empire for five centuries. When the city was overshadowed by the powerful nearby Otranto. It was only after the Norman conquest of the city that Lecce became the capital of the Salento region.

During the reign of the Normans, Tancredi, Count of Lecce and the Kingdom of the Two Sicilies, built the church of Saint Niccolò and Saint Cataldo as well as the old monastery.

In the fifteenth century Lecce became the cultural centre of Salento. It was then that the so-called Salentine Renaissance began, which saw the construction of the Castle, the city walls, a triumphal arch in honour of Emperor Charles V (now Porta Napoli), and the Ospedale dello Spirito Santo.

During the Spanish rule, Lecce became an important centre of art and culture, enriched by magnificent Baroque monuments such as the churches of Santa Teresa, Santa Chiara, Sant'Angelo, the Palazzo dei Celestini, as well as the buildings in Piazza Duomo: the Duomo, the Campanile, the Palazzo del Seminario and the Palazzo Episcopale.

The Palazzo del Seggio, better known as "il Sedile" was built in 1592, and around 1660 a Roman column was brought from Brindisi, where a statue of Saint Oronzo stands today.

In 1734, after a brief period of Austrian rule, the local nobility took power. After the Unification of Italy, the city started to expand beyond its walls and witnessed an increasing building activity, with the construction of numerous public works.

The historic centre

Porta San Biagio | Chiesa Madre di Dio | Chiesa di San Matteo

Porta San Biagio [1] - Historic centre map - C-5]

Porta San Biagio is one of the three entrances to the old quarter of Lecce and is situated on the southern side. It was built in 1774 to replace an older gate, dating back to Charles V.

The gate has double columns on either side. The coat of arms of the Bourbon king Ferdinand IV as well as those of the city are displayed above the arch. A statue representing Saint Biagio in bishop's robes stands at the top.

Chiesa Madre di Dio e di San Nicolò [2] - Historic centre map - C-5]

The Madre di Dio e di San Nicolò church, together with the adjacent Convento delle Scalze, was commissioned in 1631 by the Lecce patrician Bellissario Paladini, who wanted to transform his own house into a convent for the Barefoot Carmelites of Saint Teresa.

The façade is relatively plain, except for the elaborate portal with an ornamental carved lintel by Cesare Penna, decorated with battle motifs, such as tents, weapons, horses and foot soldiers. On either side of the portal there are niches containing the statues of the Custodian Angel and Saint Catherine of Alexandria.

The single nave has fluted pilasters with Corinthian capitals. A painting by Giovanni Andrea Coppola of the Virgin with Saint Nicholas and Saint Joseph hangs above the high altar of 1648.

Chiesa di San Matteo 3 - Historic centre map - C-5]

The church of San Matteo has more in common with the Baroque monuments of central Italy than those of Lecce.

It was built in the second half of the 17th century to a design by Achille Larducci, grandson of Francesco Borromini, who followed a style previously used by his grandfather for the façade of the Roman church of San Carlo alle Quattro Fontane.

The façade is divided in two parts: the lower is convex, decorated with scales and has an elaborate portal; the upper part is concave with two richly decorated niches.

The inside of the church is elliptical and has a single nave with arched chapels along the walls, alternating with towering statues of the Apostles.

There are various splendid altars, typical examples of Lecce's Baroque: the first one on the left has a 1813 painting of the Martyrdom of St. Agatha by Pasquale Grassi; the first one on the right, has a painting of Saint Oronzo by Serafino Elmo and the fifth on the left, a wonderful wood Pietà made in Venice in 1694.

Of particular interest is the 1691 high altar of San Matteo.

Chiesa di San Giuseppe [4 - Historic centre map - D-4]

Just off Piazza Santo Oronzo, at the corner of via Acaya and via Maremonti, is the church of San Giuseppe.

The façade has two bodies, with the statues of the Saint Anthony of Padua and Saint John of Capistriano on the sides of the lower half. There is a simple portal in the centre with a window framed by a wreath of acanthus leaves above it.

The inside has a single nave with three chapels with altars. The marble high altar displays a carved Procession of the Saints. On the left transept a fine altar of Saint Anthony of Padua is placed between those of Saint Rita and Saint Francis. On the right transept there is an eighteenth century altar dedicated to Saint Joseph with his coat of arms.

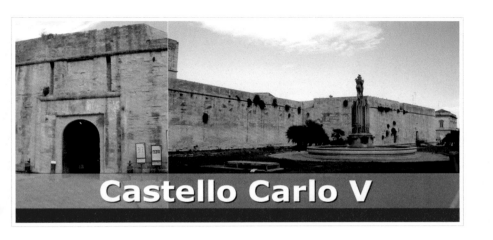

Castello Carlo V [5 - Historic centre map - D-4]

This castle was built during the reign of Charles V on the site of an previous fortress. Construction began in 1539, but it took ten years to finish the walls and the ramparts, while the interiors were completed at a later date.

At one time the castle was surrounded by a moat with its main entrance, Porta Reale, and the secondary one, Porta Falsa or Di Soccorso, protected by drawbridges. In 1872 the moat was filled in and the drawbridges removed.

Between 1870 and 1979 the castle was used by the military, and in 1983 transferred to the City of Lecce, which uses it today for cultural purposes.

Of particular artistic value is the inside 15th Century portal, which leads to the great room of the main building of the castle. This room features elegantly carved capitals and a decorated cornice.

Some parts of the Castle, such as the square tower in the centre date back to the 13th century, specifically the era of King Tancredi. The building forms a quadrangle with one bastion on each corner.

Piazza Sant'Oronzo [Historic centre map - C-4]

Piazza Sant'Oronzo is named after the patron saint of Lecce. His protection is said to have begun in 1656, when a devastating outbreak of the plague, which spread across the Kingdom of Naples, spared the city of Lecce and the Salento.

Both the people and the clergy, among them Bishop Luigi Pappacoda, were convinced that the saint had intervened to save the city from the terrible disease. It was later believed that Saint Oronzo had appeared to some people to appease them by revealing that the city would remain safe from the plague. As a consequence of this, Saint Oronzo became patron saint of Lecce.

In this historic piazza we can admire some significant and interesting monuments.

Colonna di Santo Oronzo [6 - Historic centre map - C-4]

It was originally part of a set of two pillars marking the end of the Appian Way in the city of Brindisi (where the remaining one still stands). After collapsing, and despite local opposition, it was donated by the mayor of Brindisi to the city of Lecce, where it was repaired and re-erected under the supervision of local architect Giuseppe Zimbalo. Work started in the 1660's, but took more than twenty years to complete.

A Venetian bronze statue of Saint Oronzo, designed by Mauro Manieri stands on the reconstructed Corinthian capital of the pillar and replaces the original one, which was made of wood covered with copper and was destroyed by lightning in 1737.

Anfiteatro Romano

Anfiteatro Romano [7] - Historic centre map - C-4]

The Roman amphitheatre was excavated between 1904 and 1940. Together with the Roman theatre, it testifies to the importance that the city of Lecce reached during the Roman period, specifically between the 1st and 2nd centuries AD.

Only a part of it can be seen today; the rest still lies buried beneath important secular buildings situated around the piazza.

Oval-shaped, it measures 102 metres long and 82 metres wide, with an arena of 53 by 34 metres, and could accommodate some 25.000 spectators.

Its exterior façade consisted of tufa pillars with superimposed arches, and the interior was divided into two areas of terraced seating separated from the arena by a marble-clad parapet. Sculptures of human figures fighting with wild beasts decorated the parapet.

Chiesa di San Marco | Chiesa S.M. delle Grazie | Palazzo del Sedile

Palazzo del Sedile [8 - Historic centre map - C-4]

This majestic palace was commissioned in the 16th century by mayor Pietro Mocenigo.

Its simple design combines Gothic and Renaissance elements: four square corner pillars with large pointed arches between them forming a cubic structure. Military bas-reliefs decorate the walls between the arches and the loggias above them.

The large space inside is decorated with frescoes depicting the life of Charles V. There is also a Spanish inscription from King Charles III of Spain, thanking the city of Lecce for the two pitchers of the holy oil of Saint Oronzo he had received.

Throughout the years, the building had various uses, including as town hall until 1851. It is now used for cultural purposes and as a tourist information centre.

Adjacent to this palace is the church of San Marco, built in 1543 at the behest of the thriving colony of Venetians resident in the city.

Built with local stone, the church forms a single cubic block with elaborate carved friezes that recall similar ornamental elements in the lower part of the façade of the Basilica of Santa Croce.

The tympanum contains a winged lion of Saint Mark, symbol of Venice.

Chiesa di Santa Maria delle Grazie [9 - Historic centre map - D-4]

Designed by the monk Michele Coluccio, Santa Maria delle Grazie is a Baroque church built in the late 16th century, following the discovery of a 14th century fresco of the Virgin and the Child, now preserved inside.

The façade is divided vertically into three parts framed by Corinthian columns and pilasters. The richly decorated central portal is surmounted by an arched tympanum and a window adorned with a balustrade.

On the sides there are four niches, two in the lower half, which hold statues of Saint Peter and Saint Paul, and two empty ones in the upper half.

The Latin cross interior has a walnut coffered ceiling and a wooden crucifix, both by Vespasiano Genuino da Gallipoli, as well as a paintings by local painter Oronzo Tiso of the Assumption of the Virgin, the Adoration of the Shepherds and Saint Michael the Archangel.

Chiesa di Santa Irene [10 - Historic centre map - C-4]

The construction of this church started in 1591, based on a design by Francesco Grimaldi, which recalls that of Sant'Andrea della Valle in Rome. It is dedicated to Saint Irene of Lecce, patron saint of the city until 1656, when she was replaced by Saint Oronzo.

Its façade is divided in two orders or halves, each subdivided into various sections separated by Corinthian columns and pilasters. A statue of Saint

17

Irene by Manieri presides over the central portal, and above it, the coat of arms of the city of Lecce.

The inside of the church follows the Latin cross pattern. On either side of the single nave there are three interconnecting chapels with elliptical domed ceilings.

A series of elaborate baroque and rococo altars can be seen in these chapels, as well as on either side of the transept.

Of particular interest is Oronzo Tiso's masterpiece "The Transportation of the Holy Ark", which hangs above the main altar.

Piazza Duomo [Historic centre map - B-4]

Not far from the church of Sant'Irene, in the direction of via Vittorio Emanuele II, which connects with via G. Libertini, we reach, Piazza del Duomo.

The Campanile, the Duomo, the Palazzo Vescovile and the Palazzo del Seminario, are all situated around this magnificent piazza, forming an enclosure with one single entrance.

Campanile — Duomo

Campanile [**11** - Historic centre map - B-4]

The 72 meter high square bell tower, built between 1661 and 1682 by local architect Giuseppe Zimbalo, consists of five stories, each smaller in width an height than the previous one. The upper floors have lancet windows and balconies with balustrades, running around all four walls, which are decorated with Latin epigraphs by Giovanni Camillo Palma.

An iron statue of Saint Oronzo stands on top of the majolica tiled dome.

Duomo [**12** - Historic centre map - B-4]

The construction of the first cathedral began in 1144 under bishop Formoso. In 1659 bishop Pappacoda called on Gustavo Zimbalo, who was already in charge of the construction of the campanile, to restore the Duomo.

Facing the entrance to the square, the left hand side of the cathedral presents a richly decorated 17th century portal crowned by a statue of

Saint Oronzo. On either side of the portal are the statues of Saint Giusto and Saint Fortunato.

The main façade is more sober and is decorated with flutes pilasters and niches containing the statues of Saint Peter, Saint Paul, Saint Gennaro and Saint Louis of Toulouse.

The Latin cross shaped interior is divided into three naves by pillars and half-columns. In addition to the high altar there are twelve more altars along the naves and transept.

A finely carved wood ceiling covers the central aisle and transept, and displays gilded framed scenes of the life of Saint Oronzo by Giuseppe da Brindisi.

The superb marble and gilded bronze high altar is devoted to the Assumption of the Virgin Mary, depicted in a large central painting by Antonio Tiso.

A large number of paintings by G. Dominico Catalano are displayed in the sacristy and adjacent chapter house.

The Duomo also houses a fine walnut choir made in 1758 by Emanuele Manieri.

Palazzo Vescovile [13] - Historic centre map - B-4]

This palace was commissioned by Girolamo Guidano, Bishop of Lecce between 1420 and 1425. It was enlarged in 1649 by Bishop Pappacoda, who had the right wing guest rooms built.

The baroque façade dates back to 1758 on a design by Manieri. The portal stands on a rusticated basement displaying the coat of arms of Bishop Carafa. On the upper side, there are three niches containing statues, the central one representing the Virgin Mary, and, above them, a 1761 clock by Dominico Panico.

The palace is home to the state apartments, the bishop's residence and the offices of the Diocesan curia. The gallery displays a statue of the Assumption and paintings by Catalano and Giordano.

Palazzo del Seminario [14] - Historic centre map - B-4]

The Palazzo del Seminario is one of the most important Baroque monuments of Puglia. It was commissioned by bishop Pignatelli and built between 1694 and 1709 by Giuseppe Cino.

The monumental façade is divided into two sections, the lower half consisting of two floors with sixteen richly decorated windows, and a simpler more linear upper third floor, designed by Manieri. The central portal is surmounted by a balcony with a three-arched window.

The courtyard leads to the private chapel of the seminary, and contains a famous well, exuberantly decorated, known as "Vera Ovale", attributed to Giuseppe Cino.

Chiesa di Santa Teresa [15 - Historic centre map - B-4]

Originally attached to a convent of Carmelitane nuns established in 1620, its construction was entrusted to Giuseppe Zimbalo.

The unfinished façade has eight fluted Corinthian columns and two niches with the statues of Saint John the Baptist and Saint John the Evangelist. The upper half is adorned with floral motifs.

The interior consists on a single nave with side chapels and three altars on either side. On the left hand side, the altar of Saint Teresa is by Zimbalo.

The presbytery contains the old wood choir and various religious paintings.

A large papier mâché figure of Saint Oronzo stands above the main entrance.

Chiesa di S. Anna | Convento Chiesa S. Anna | Chiesa S. G. Battista

Chiesa di Sant'Anna ed il Conservatorio

[**16** - Historic centre map - B-4]

The church of Sant'Anna is a small but elegant baroque church built in 1680. It has a simple architectural structure and a design similar to the Duomo.

Its façade is composed of two orders crowned by a pediment. In the lower order the portal is flanked by two niches housing statues of Saint Peter and Saint Paul. On the cornice above it there is a bust of Saint Anne and two small angels. The upper order follows a similar design, with a large central window and two niches with statues of Saint Andrew and Saint John the Evangelist.

Inside, a single nave contains four chapels with 18th century paintings.

A notable feature is the carved wood ceiling, which displays the coats of arms of the noble families of the girls who lived in the adjacent conservatory. A painting of Saint Anne by Stano decorates the main altar.

The adjacent Conservatory of Sant'Anna opened in 1686, as a home to ladies from the local aristocracy, who were the only ones allowed to reside there. It was restored, enlarged and embellished by Manieri in 1764.

Chiesa di San Giovanni Battista al Rosario

[17 - Historic centre map - A-4]

This church was built between 1691 and 1728 on a design by Zimbalo. It was declared a minor basilica by Pope Pius XII in 1948.

The façade has two bodies divided by a balustrade, with a central statue of the Virgin, decorated with flower trophies, that represent the visions of the prophet Ezekiel.

The lower body consists of two tall fluted columns flanking a large portal with the emblem of the Dominicans and a statue of Saint Dominic. On either side of the portal there are two niches with statues of saints.

The Greek cross shaped interior has a large octagonal space in the centre, where the coats of arms of the families who contributed to its construction are carved at the base of the pillars. The entire inner perimeter is marked by thirteen altars with niches containing statues of saints.

A picture of John the Baptist preaching, by 17th century painter Oronzo Letizia hangs on the wall behind the main altar, together with a few other religious paintings.

Of particular interest is the pulpit, which is decorated with scenes from the Apocalypse, and is the sole example in Lecce completely made of the local stone.

Convento dei Domenicani [18 - Historic centre map - A-4]

The Convento dei Domenicani, located on the side of the church of San Giovanni Battista, was founded in the fourteenth century by Giovanni D'Aymo for the Dominican friars.

Later the property was rebuilt, starting in the late 17th century by Zimbalo, and after his death, by Manieri, who completed the project in the 18th century, adding the cloister, the upper rooms and the simple façade with its two fine portals surmounted by balconies.

It is now the headquarters of the Accademia delle Belle Arti.

Porta Rudiae [19 - Historic centre map - A-4]

Porta Rudiae is the oldest and most interesting of the city gates. In ancient times, this road lead to the long vanished city of Rudiae.

Also known as Porta Sant'Oronzo, after the statue of the saint which stands at the top, the gate was rebuilt in 1703, the original having collapsed at the end of the 17th century. It consists of a single arch with two sets of columns on either side. Above them, there are four busts representing the legendary founders of the city: Malennius, Daunus, Euippa and Idomeneus, as well as statues of Saint Irene and Saint Dominic.

Palazzo Marrese [20 - Historic centre map - B-3]

The Palazzo Marrese is an elegant palace located in the charming piazzetta Falconieri. It has a façade divided into two sections by means of a cornice resting on anthropomorphic corbels, which doubles as a balcony.

Of great beauty, the portal is framed by four pilasters that become caryatids supporting the cornice. The upper floor has simple windows with pediments containing busts.

Palazzo Palmieri [21 - Historic centre map - B-3]

Palazzo Palmieri has two façades dating from different periods: the one facing via Palmieri is 16th century and the one facing piazzetta Falconieri, with its intricate rococo balconies, 17th century.

Inside the palace, a staircase carved into the rock leads down to an underground corridor, decorated with a bas-relief frieze.

An inscription on the lintel of the door marks the entrance to a

Messapian hypogeum, probably intended to contain the tombs of a local aristocratic family of the 4th - 3rd centuries BC.

Palazzo Palmieri represent, in fact, one of the examples documenting the presence of intramural burial spaces in the ancient town of Lupiae, before the Roman occupation.

Teatro Paisiello 22 - Historic centre map - B-3]

With its elegant neoclassical façade and jewel-box interior, the Teatro Paisiello is a classic example of the Italian style theatres that were popular toward the end of the 16th century and beginning of the 17th century. Its 320 seats and small stage, make it more suited to prose, concerts or ballet, than to large scale spectacles, such as opera.

The current theatre dates back to 1872 by Oronzo Bernardini and replaces a previous one built in wood on the site of the former armoury. Originally called "Teatro Nuovo", it was later renamed after Apulian composer Giovanni Paisiello.

The theatre also owns a piano which belonged to the famous local tenor Tito Schipa.

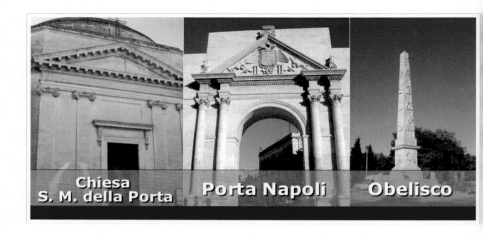

Chiesa S. M. della Porta

Porta Napoli

Obelisco

Chiesa di Santa Maria della Porta [23 - Historic centre map - B-3]

Situated in the vicinity of Porta Napoli, the Chiesa di Santa Maria della Porta was originally a small chapel outside the city walls. It was later enlarged and rebuilt at various times, most recently between 1852 and 1858, when it adored its present octagonal shape and neoclassical exterior.

The main façade has a portal flanked by two pairs of Doric columns topped by a large tympanum the length of the façade.

Inside the church, four large arches support the dome, whereas four smaller ones lead into two rectangular chapels with barrel vaulted ceilings next to the entrance and two semicircular chapels at both sides of the apse.

Porta Napoli [24 - Historic centre map - B-3]

Porta Napoli is a triumphal arch-like structure built in honour of Charles

V, who was responsible for the construction of the defensive fortifications of the city. As its name indicates, it originally marked the start of the road to Naples.

Now free-standing, the single arch is flanked by two sets of Corinthian columns supporting a tympanum, which displays the coat of arms of the Habsburgs. A Latin epigraph under the cornice praises Charles V, victorious against the Turks.

Obelisco [25 - Historic centre map - B-2]

This obelisk was erected in 1822 by Vito Carluccio during a visit to Lecce by King Ferdinand I of the Two Sicilies.

The Obelisk is placed on a platform and decorated on its four sides with bas-reliefs. The pedestal has the coat of arms of the province of Terra d'Otranto: a dolphin biting a Turkish crescent.

Chiesa delle Alcantarine [26 - Historic centre map - C-2]

The popular name of this church recalls a former monastery of Alcantarine Franciscan nuns attached to it. Its official name is actually chiesa di Santa Maria della Provvidenza. It was designed in the early 18th century by Giuseppe Cino and later modified and finished in 1744 by Manieri.

The main façade is divided into three sections. The first has four niches interspread with half-flat, half-fluted pilasters. The niches contain statues of Saint Raphael the Archangel, Saint Anthony of Padua, Saint Francis d'Assisi and Saint Michael the Archangel. The second section has a large window and two side niches with sculptures of San Peter of Alcantara and Saint Pascal Baylon. The upper section consists of a classical pediment with two pine cones on each corner.

The inside of the church has a single nave with three chapels on each side. Presiding the first two, left and right, are depictions of the Crucifixion and the Madonna and Child. The presbytery contains a painting of the Adoration of the Shepherds by Diego Bianchi and two statues by Manieri.

Chiesa di Santa Maria degli Angeli

[27 - Historic centre map - C-2]

The construction of this church, disposed in his will by Florentine nobleman Bernando Peruzzi, began in 1524. Later modifications have altered its original appearance. It was once attached to Franciscan monastery, which today houses a military barrack.

The relatively simple façade preserves an elaborate renaissance portal, with two intricately carved columns and a frieze sustaining a tympanum with a statue of the Virgin Mary and Child by Zimbalo. On either side there are two large baroque windows

Renovation work in the interior during the 18th century saw the stucco cladding of the three naves, including the columns; the replacement of the flooring and the addition of side altars and a statue of Saint Michael the Archangel.

Chiesa di S.G. Evangelista
[28 - Historic centre map - C-2]

The church of San Giovanni Evangelista and its adjoining Benedictine monastery were once under direct papal jurisdiction. Although it dates back to the 12th century, little remains of the original structure, which reflects a mixture of styles.

The tapered façade has a large arched entrance and a statue of Saint Benedict in a niche.

The single nave interior is predominantly baroque, with a striking coffered wood ceiling; a majolica tiled floor; a rococo pulpit and a series of altars from the 17th and 18th centuries.

An imposing bell tower was added in the early 16th century.

Chiesa di Sant'Angelo   [29 - Historic centre map - C-2]

The church of San Angelo is one of the oldest churches in the city, dating back to 1061. It was originally located outside the city walls, until these where extended during the reign of Charles V.

In 1663, due to poor structural conditions it was decided to rebuild it in the style of the period.

The unfinished façade is divided into five parts by large Corinthian pillars and pilasters, with empty niches between them. The bronze doors were created by Emanuele Manieri 1750. The portal is surmounted by a semicircular tympanum supporting a statue of the Virgin and Child.

The Latin cross shaped interior has three naves and four chapels on either side, that house richly decorated altars with helical columns, statues and friezes.

The high altar, situated in the presbytery, is devoted to the Our Lady of Constantinople.

Chiesa Greca [30 - Historic centre map - C-3]

Officially Chiesa di San Nicolò, it is generally referred to as Chiesa Greca or Greek Church, as it has been used, for centuries, by the Greco-Albanian community residing in the city.

The current church was built in 1765, based on designs by four architects of the time: Francesco Palma, Lazzaro Marsione, Lazzaro Lombardo and Vincenzo Carrozzo.

The simple façade is divided into three parts by a double row of pilasters. A cornice separates the portal from a mixtilinear window high above it. The interior of the hall church is reminiscent that of Greco-Byzantine churches.

Palazzo Adorno [31 - Historic centre map - C-3]

Designed by Gabriele Riccardi in 1565, Palazzo Adorno was commissioned by Gabriele Adorno, commander of Charles V's Imperial Navy.

The most characteristic element is its bevelled bossage on the exterior walls, which becomes diamond-shaped in the entrance hall and staircase. The entrance hall is also profusely decorated with anthropomorphic sculptures and floral and geometric designs.

The coat of arms of the Personè, former inhabitants of the palace, is displayed above the entrance.

The building is now the headquarters of the Provincial Administration.

Convento dei Celestini

Chiesa S. Croce

Convento dei Celestini [32 - Historic centre map - C-3]

In 1549, the original Convent of the Celestini was demolished to make room for the enlarging and strengthening of the castle walls, ordered by Charles V. Consequently, the monks moved the monastery to its current location, where they remained for the next 300 years. It now houses the offices of the Prefecture and the Province of Lecce.

It was started in 1549 by Riccardi, who designed the cloister, with its 24 arches and 44 columns, and the lower section of the adjacent Basilica di Santa Croce. A century later, the building was completed by Zimbalo and Cino, who designed, receptively, the first and second levels of the façade.

A large number of richly decorated windows separated by pilasters and two small loggias on either side embellish the façade. The central portal is decorated with cherubs and fruit garlands.

Basilica di Santa Croce [33 - Historic centre map - C-3]

The Basilica of Santa Croce is usually considered the best example of the "Barocco leccese". Gabriele Riccardi was in charge of the first phase of its construction, which began in 1549 and took some 150 years to complete. Various other architects left their mark on the building, such as Francesco Antonio Zimbalo, who added the portals; Cesare Penna, who designed the magnificent rose window and Giuseppe Zimbalo, who completed the extravagant decoration of the upper half.

The lower half of the façade is divided into five sections by six columns, which support a richly decorated entablature. The coats of arms of Philip III of Spain, Mary of Eghien and Walter VI of Brienne are displayed above the central portal. The entablature is surmounted by a series of atlantes, lions and mythological creatures, which support a balustrade decorated with cherubs.

The upper half is dominated by the giant rose window adorned with floral motifs, and a niche on each side containing the statues of Saint Benedict and Pope Celestine V. At the far ends, there are female figures representing faith and charity.

Inside, the Latin-cross layout had originally five naves, the two outer ones having later been transformed into side chapels. The central nave has a superb gilded walnut coffered ceiling, whereas the aisles have cross vaults. The crossing is surmounted by a windowed dome, decorated with cherubs and floral motifs.

The chancel, devoid of its original wood choir and high altar, ends in a polylobulated apse. The current high altar was brought here from the church of Santi Niccolò e Cataldo in 1956. Particularly relevant, among the many other altars in the church, is the one dedicated to Saint Fancis of Paola, a masterpiece by Francesco Antonio Zimbalo.

Arco di Prato [34 - Historic centre map - C-3]

This arch forms a deep archway entrance to the Palazzo del Prato. The simple decoration consists of weather worn fluted pilasters and a loggia with a balustrade.

A local legend tells the story of former owner Leonardo Prato, who obtained for his palace the right of asylum from Charles V. This prevented anybody who walked in through the archway from being arrested.

Chiesa del Gesù 35 - Historic centre map - C-3]

Commissioned by the recently arrived Jesuits, building started in 1575, on the site of the small ancient church of San Niccolò dei Greci, which had to be demolished. Giovanni De Rossi followed a design similar to that of the order's mother church in Rome.

Outside, the linear façade is divided into two bodies by a cornice. The statue of a pelican feeding its young, symbol of the order, stands at the top of the broken pediment.

The Latin-cross shaped interior has a single nave with two interconnecting chapels on each side. The wood ceiling displays scenes depicting the Glories of the Society of Jesus by Giuseppe Brindisi.

Situated in the presbytery, behind the wood choir, is the spectacular high altar created by Giuseppe Cino in 1699, using the local stone. It combines impressive columns and statues of the Evangelists on corbels, with religious paintings by Oratio Letizia and Oronzo Liso.

Palazzo Carafa 36 - Historic centre map - C-3]

Palazzo Carafa stands on a site that had been occupied by a convent of Paolette (Franciscan) nuns since 1542. In 1764, bishop Sozy-Carafa comissioned Emanuele Manieri to design a new building to replace the old convent.

Later in 1893, the city took over the building and adapted the interior spaces for use as Town Hall, adding the portal with the Carafa coat of arms and the surmounting balcony.

The façade alternates Corinthian smooth pilasters running the entire height of the building, with windows decorated with mixtilinear pediments.

Chiesa di S. Chiara | Teatro Romano | Chiesa del Carmine

Chiesa di Santa Chiara [37 - Historic centre map - C-4]

The original 15th century church of Santa Chiara was rebuilt at the end of the 17th century by Giuseppe Cino.

Its convex façade was never completed and is divided into two sections. The splendid portal is surmounted by the coat of arms of the Clarisses and surrounded by empty niches decorated with medallions.

The octagonal interior is equally divided into two sections by a cornice running along the walls. Below, there are three chapels on each side separated by Corinthian pilasters. Above, seven windows alternate with statues in niches.

Notable works of art include the monumental high altar in the presbytery, and a Saint Agnes by Francesco Solimena in the sacristy.

Teatro Romano [38 - Historic centre map - C-4]

Dating back to the reign of Augustus, the remains of Lecce's Roman theatre were rediscovered and excavated in 1929.

The theatre is 40 meters wide and divided into six sections of terraces by five stairways. In the orchestra area, three larger terraces were reserved for the authorities. These are separated from the rest by a small wall. The theatre had an estimated capacity for 5.000 spectators.

In front of the 30 meter wide stage, a narrow channel where the curtain would rest can still be seen.

Some of the statues which decorated the theatre have been retrieved, and are displayed at the Museo Provinciale Sigismondo Castromediano.

Chiesa del Carmine [39 - Historic centre map - B-5]

The construction of the Chiesa del Carmine, adjacent to the convent of the Carmelites, was begun in 1714 by Cino who worked on it until his death in 1722. It was then completed by Emanuele Manieri in 1737.

The façade of the church is divided into three sections, the lower two decorated with garlands and niches containing statues of saints by Manieri. The portal has a curved tympanum with an image of Our Lady of Carmel.

The interior layout mimics the shape of a human foot, with biblical connotations. On each side of the nave there are three chapels with baroque altars by Manieri. The dome above the presbytery is covered in white and green majolica tiles.

Behind the main altar there is a fine choir with a series of religious paintings by Serafino Elmo.

Chiesa dei S.S. Niccolò e Cataldo

[40 - Historic centre map - A-1]

The church of Saint Niccolò and Saint Cataldo, along with the adjoining Benedictine monastery, was founded in 1180 by the last Norman king, Tancredi d'Altavilla.

In 1494, the complex was taken over by the Olivetan congregation, who undertook a series of renovations.

The façade combines original Romanesque elements, such as the portal and the rose window, with later baroque additions by Giuseppe Cino, such as a series of stone statues of saints and a square pediment with the coat of arms of the Olivetans.

On the right hand side of the church there is a 16th century cloister by Riccardi, and on the left the nineteenth-century section of Lecce's cemetery.

The interior has a basilica-based design with three naves separated by quadrilobulate pillars. The vaulted ceilings are entirely covered in bright-coloured frescoes.

Some of the altars along the aisles are attributed to Manieri.

Museums

Museo Archeologico Provinciale Sigismondo Castromediano

This is the oldest archaeological museum in Puglia. It covers the history of the region from ancient times, like the reconstructed prehistoric cave of Grotta dei Cervi in Porto Badisco, all the way to the 20th century.

The displays include many archaeological finds from Messapian, Greek and Roman settlements, such as Rudiae, Roca Vecchia and from the territories of Bari and Brindisi: vases, pottery, bronzes, inscriptions, sculptures and other artefacts.

The medieval and baroque sections document the Byzantine and Venetian influences on the work of local artists from the Middle Ages until the 18th century and include a collection of Murano glass and Venetian paintings. A final section is devoted to the 19th and 20th centuries.

Open from 9.00 to 13.00 and from 14.30 to 19.30, Monday to Sunday.

Closed on Sunday afternoon and holidays.
Admission free.

Viale Gallipoli, 28 [Historic centre map - C-6]
Telephone: +39 0832 683503

Museo Storico Archeologico (MUSA)

The MUSA is an exhibition space set up to highlight and promote, in a didactic way, the results of researches made by archaeologists and historians of the Salento University in the last decades.

The exhibits cover the main stages of the course of research campaigns carried out by archaeologists and historians, whilst presenting an up-to-date outlook of the latest research developments in the Salento area, from prehistoric times to the Middle Ages.

Open from 09.00 to 13.30, Monday to Friday and from 15.00 to 17.30, Tuesday and Thursday.
Admission free.

Via di Valesio [Historic centre map - B-2]
Telephone: +39 0832 455008

Museo Storico della città di Lecce (MUST)

The MUST is located in the heart of the historical centre of Lecce, next to the church of Santa Chiara and the ancient Roman Theatre.

At the entrance of this museum there is a large room that houses a contemporary art gallery with a permanent exhibition of the works by the sculptor Cosimo Salento Carlucci.

On the first floor, a series of rooms display exhibits from the various periods of the history of Lecce: from Messapian and Roman times, the Middle Ages, all the way to the 20th century.

Open from 10.00 to 13.00 and from 15.00 to 19.00, Tuesday to Sunday and from 15.00 to 23.00 Saturdays.

Closed on Thursday, 25 of December 25 and 1 January.
Admission free.

Via degli Ammirati, 11 [Historic centre map - C-4]
Telephone: +39 0832 682988

Museo Diocesano di Arte Sacra

This museum, located in the Palazzo del Seminario in Piazza Duomo, was founded with the aim to preserve and protect the works of art from religious institutions.

The paintings on display span a period from the end of the 15th century to the end of the 18th century. Other exhibits include sculptures and silver objects, such as chalices and censers, many of which were part of the liturgical treasure of the Duomo of Lecce, and date back to the 17th and 18th centuries.

Open from 9.30 to 12.30 and from 16.00 to 19.00 (Winter), and from 9.30 to 12.30 and from 17.00 to 20.00 (Summer).

Closed on Sundays and Monday and Friday in the afternoon.

Piazza Duomo, 11 [Historic centre map - B-4]
Telephone: +39 0832 244764

Museo del Teatro Romano

Adjoining the ancient Roman Theatre, this museum displays findings from archaeological excavations carried out at the beginning of the last century.

It also holds an exhibition entitled "Rome. The scene of life" in collaboration with the Sovrintendenza Archeologica of Rome and the Sovrintendenza Archelogica of Puglia, on the theme of stage design and the use of illusion to represent reality in the Roman world.

Open from 09.30 to 13.00, Monday to Saturday.
Afternoons by appointment only.

Via degli Ammirati [Historic centre map - C-4]
Telephone: +39 0832 279196

Mostra Permanente dell'Artigianato Salentino

This permanent exhibition displays artefacts by local craftspeople of the Salento, using materials such as papier mâché, pietra leccese (the soft local stone), ceramic or wrought iron.

Open from 9.00 to 13.00 and from 16.30 to 20.00.
Admission free.

Via Rubichi 21 [Historic centre map - C-4]
Telephone: +39 0832 246758

Pinacoteca d'Arte Francescana e Biblioteca Caracciolo

This picture gallery is located in the 16th century Palazzo Fulgenzio. It displays hundreds of paintings, mostly by anonymous monks from the Franciscan convents of Puglia and particularly of the Salento.

Most works of art belong to the historical period between the 17th and 18th centuries, namely that of the Baroque and the Catholic Counter-Reformation.

Open from 9.00 to 12.00, Monday to Friday and from 16.00 to 18.30, Monday, Wednesday and Friday.

Closed on Saturday, Sunday and August.
Admission free.

Via Imperatore Adriano, 79 [Historic centre map - D-3]
Telephone: +39 0832 455008

Museo Papirologico

The Museo Papirologico was created to house the University of Salento's collection of Greek, Hieroglific, Demotic, Hieratic and Coptic papyri, in addition to more than 400 artefacts on the theme of writing in ancient times.

Open from 9.00 to 13.00, Monday to Friday and from 9.00 to 13.00 and 15.00-18.00, Monday and Thursday.

Admission Free.

Via Di Valesio [Historic centre map - B-2]
Tel: +39 0832 294457 - +39 0832 294459

Museo Faggiano

This museum, situated in the historical centre of Lecce, was created only a few years ago, after the accidental discovery, during renovation works, of archaeological remains dating back more than 2000 years.

The excavations in the basement revealed circular holes cut into the bedrock for the erection of huts, as well as various cisterns from the 15th and 16th centuries and a 10 meter deep well, which draws water from an underground river.

Open from 9.30 to 13.00 and from 16.00 to 20.00.

Via Ascanio Grandi, 56 [Historic centre map - C-4/5]
Telephone: +39 0832 300528

Theatres

Teatro Comunale Giovanni Paisiello

Via Giuseppe Palmieri, 10 [Historic centre map - B-3]
Telephone: +39 0832 245499 or +39 0832 682104

Teatro Politeama Greco

Via XXV Luglio, 30 [Historic centre map - D-3]
Telephone: +39 0832 241468

Roman Amphitheatre

Open from 10.30 to 12.00 and from 17.00 to 19.00, April, May and
September and from 18.00 to 20.00, June, July and August.
Shows during the summer only.

Piazza Sant'Oronzo [Historic centre map - C-4]
Telephone: +39 0832 253791 - +39 0832 246517

Roman Theatre

Open from 09.30 to 13.00, Monday to Saturday afternoons and public
holidays by appointment only.

Access sightseeing: via Ammirati - Museum of the Roman Theatre of the Fondazione Memmo.

Via del Teatro Romano [Historic centre map - C-4]
Telephone: +39 0832 253791

Annual events

Feast of Saint Oronzo

The festivity of the Patron Saint of Lecce, Saint Oronzo, is a three day celebration, from 24th to 26th August, which consists of a series of religious and popular events.

The religious festivities start on the afternoon of 24th August, with a gathering, in front of the Duomo of Lecce, of the faithful, the various religious brotherhoods and representatives of the most important local governments. Afterwards, a long procession takes place through the streets of the town.

During the three days of festivities, masses in honour of the saint are celebrated and the council organizes various kinds of shows.

Open courtyards

This is a popular event held in May in the historic centre of Lecce, when most of the beautiful courtyards, which are scattered around the old town, are exceptionally open to the public.

European Film Festival

This is a one week film festival which usually takes place in April. The Ulivo dOro prize is awarded to international film makers and actors in the course of the closing day ceremony.

Puglia Open Days Winter

Many towns in Puglia, including Lecce, have Open Days between the months of November and January, usually on weekends, when many important monuments are exceptionally open to the public, with guided tours, exhibitions and free activities.

2. The surroundings

Archaeological sites

Parco Archeologico di Rudiae [Territory map - B-4]

The Archaeological Park of Rudiae is situated on the site of an ancient Messapian and Roman city located just 3 km from Lecce. It is an area of great historical, cultural and archaeological interest.

The remains of an amphitheatre, part of the city walls, numerous chamber tombs, a pit and underground rooms can be visited.

Many of the findings of this archaeological site, such as glass fragments, relics and ornaments are now preserved at the Museo Sigismondo Castromediano.

How to get there

The site is located near the via Vecchia Cupertino direction south-west, SS 16 San Pietro in Lama.

GPS coordinates

Latitude: 40.333781 (40° 20' 1.6")
Longitude: 18.147284 (18° 8' 50.2")

Monasteries

Abbazia di Santa Maria di Cerrate [Territory map - B-3]

The Abbazia di Cerrate, located between Torre Rinalda and Casalabate, is a Romanesque monastery, built by Tancredi d'Altavilla, Count of Lecce, in the 12th century.

It is considered one of the most important medieval monuments in Puglia for its distinct architectural decoration and the many frescoes, which once completely covered its interior walls.

The façade has a 13th century portal surmounted by an arch with bas-reliefs depicting scenes from the New Testament. On either side of the portal there is a lancet window and, above it, a small rose window.

On the left hand side of the temple there is a fine 13th century portico with cilindrical and polygonal columns and decorated capitals. In front of the portico there is a Renaissance well.

The interior is decorated with 13th and 14th century frescoes, some of which have been restored and moved to a nearby museum.

The Abbey is currently managed by the Italian Environmental Fund, which acquired the property in 2012.

How to get there

The Abbey is located along the SP 100, from Casalabate to Squinzano.

GPS coordinates

Latitude: 40.458631 (40° 27' 31")
Longitude: 18.115438 (18° 6' 55")

Nature reserves

Parco Regionale Boschi e Paludi di Rauccio
[Territory map - B-3]

This park, located some 6 km from Lecce, is all that is left from a vast wooded area that once surrounded the city.

The park covers about 600 acres, and includes a wetland, two coastal basins (Idume and Fetida), along with three canals (Rauccio, Gelsi and Fetida). The remaining part of the territory is occupied by Mediterranean vegetation and large agricultural and uncultivated areas.

Today, the appearance of the park is the result of both the profound changes made by man over the centuries, so that the area could be used for agricultural purposes, and the adaptation of vegetation to constantly changing environmental conditions.

Rare species of plants and animals can also be found, which make the park of Rauccio a site to visit for anyone interested in nature and its preservation.

The Management Authority of the park has entrusted exclusively to Terradimezzo the educational, recreational and tourist activities for the whole area.

Operational Headquarters: Via Silvio Pellico, 35 – Lecce
Latitude: 40.359088 (40° 21' 32.7162")
Longitude: 18.159101 (18° 9' 32.763")
Telephone: +39 0832 302297
(Ony Monday and Friday from 17.00 to 20.00)
Mobile: +39 328 541 2181
Email: terradimezzo.coop@tiscali.it
Website: www.coopterradimezzo.it

How to get there

Take the SP 131 from Lecce to Torre Chianca. After 6 km turn left at the Masseria Ospitale, after 2 km turn left again into via Masseria Rauccio and follow the signs.

GPS coordinates

Latitude: 40.456500 (40° 27' 23.4")
Longitude: 18.167000 (18° 10' 01.2")

Oasi Naturalistica Bacino Costiero Acquatina
[Territory map - C-3]

The nature reserve of Acquatina is a wetland situated along the coast near Frigole. The place was known in Norman times as the "Guadina", a marshy area periodically flooded by storm surges, but rich in numerous fish species.

In the early 1900's, maintenance and restoration work of the marshland took place, which included the construction of a wall to contain the brackish water, thus permanently altering the landscape.

The Bacino of Acquatina is connected to the sea by a long shallow canal on the south side, and is also supplied with freshwater from the Giammateo canal on the north side.

In common with other wetlands along the coast, the Oasi is surrounded by the typical Mediterranean vegetation of the area and has a rich diversity of fish, crustaceans, molluscs, as well as aquatic plants and algae, which also makes it an ideal home for local and migrating birds.

How to get there

It is accessible by private vehicle or by bus, following the SP133, which leaves from the SP 131, that goes from Lecce to Torre Chianca.

GPS coordinates

Latitude: 40.443251 (40° 26' 35.7")
Longitude: 18.236923 (18° 14' 12.9")

Bacino dell'Idume [Territory map - B-2]

The Bacino of the Idume is an artificial pond situated along the coast, between Frigole and Torre Chianca. It was created during drainage works to collect the water from a number of channelled watercourses including the River Idume. Apart from underwater vegetation and algae, the pond is surrounded by a great variety of plant species, such as reeds and daffodils, among others.

How to get there

To get there take the SP 131 and, turning at the SP 133, follow signs to Torre Rinalda for a few kilometers.

GPS coordinates

Latitude: 40.466893 (40° 28' 0.8")
Longitude: 18.187141 (18° 11' 13.7")

Riserva Naturale San Cataldo [Territory map - D-4]

The San Cataldo Nature Reserve is a 28 hectare protected area, which was set up in 1977 by the Ministry of Agriculture. Originally a malaria infested swampland, it was gradually drained during the 20th century. Fast growing species of trees, such as pines and eucalyptus, were also planted, thus changing the character and appearance of the area.

In addition to a rich variety of Mediterranean plant species, the Reserve is also home to numerous animals, such as foxes, hedgehogs, badgers or weasels, as well as many types of reptiles and birds.

How to get there

The reserve is located to the south of San Cataldo. To get there take the SP 364 to San Cataldo and head south.

GPS coordinates

Latitude: 40.382736 (40° 22' 57.8")
Longitude: 18.304386 (18° 18' 15.7")

Riserva naturale dello Stato Le Cesine
[Territory map - D-4]

This nature area, managed and protected by the WWF, is one of the last stretches of marshes that once extended between Brindisi and Otranto. It is an area with different natural habitats, dunes, wetlands, drainage canals, mixed forest and Mediterranean vegetation. There are also two ponds, Salapi and Pantano Grande, fed by rainwater and separated from the sea by a strip of sand dunes.

The reserve is home to unusual plants and numerous species of birds. Currently it includes 380 of the 620 acres of wetland in the area and is located by 'Le Cesine' farmhouse, used as a guest and visitor centre.

The Reserve is open all year round.

Tours are held on Sundays and public holidays at the following times:

from 1 October to 31 May starting at 10.30
from 1 June to 30 September starting at 16.30

During the summer there are guided visits on weekdays. Groups and schools can visit the oasis daily, by appointment.

Bird watching is possible during certain periods.

Entrance

SP San Cataldo - San Foca
Masseria Cesine - 73029 Vernole (Le)
Telephone: +39 329 8315714
Website: www.riservalecesine.it

How to get there

From Lecce, take the main road to San Cataldo. Arriving there, turn right at the first traffic light towards Otranto. At about 2.8 km, the entrance is marked with a WWF flag. Follow the road for about 1 km to the visitor centre of Masseria Le Cesine.

GPS coordinates

Latitude: 40.350692 (40° 21' 2.4")
Longitude: 18.341122 (18° 20' 28")

Beaches

There are several seaside resorts along the coast of the territory of Lecce.

San Cataldo [Territory map - D-3/4]

San Cataldo is one of the most famous and popular beaches in Lecce as well as being a pleasant port town. During the reign of Roman emperor Hadrian the port was important for trade with the East. Near the lighthouse, the archaeological remains of the ancient "Porto Adriano" can still be seen.

How to get there

Take the SP 364 from the exit 8B of the ring road.

GPS coordinates

Latitude: 40.389666 (40° 23' 22.7")
Longitude: 18.304558 (18° 18' 16.4")

Frigole [Territory map - C-3]

Frigole has one of the most beautiful coastlines of the area, with its white sandy beaches and crystal clear waters and the gorgeous Salento landscape as a backdrop. The beach is almost entirely equipped with lido facilities. There is also a small port for boats, home of the Lega Navale Italiana.

How to get there

Take the exit 4B from the ring road.

GPS coordinates

Latitude: 40.428486 (40° 25' 42.5")
Longitude: 18.248425 (18° 14' 54.3")

Torre Chianca [Territory map - C-3]

Torre Chianca takes its name from the ancient coastal tower, now partly in ruins, built by the Spaniards to defend the territory. A small islet, locally known as "lu squieu" (the rock), forms part of the resort.

Apart from its bathing lidos, the area is also famous for the archaeological remains preserved in its waters, such as a series of marble columns dating back to the second century BC.

How to get there

Take the exit 3 to Torre Chianca from the ring road.

GPS coordinates

Latitude: 40.463628 (40° 27' 49")
Longitude: 18.201904 (18° 12' 6.8")

Torre Rinalda [Territory map - B-2]

Torre Rinalda, which derives its name from a semi-ruined watchtower, is a typical coastal resort with long beaches and clear waters. There are private lidos along the beach as well as public access stretches of sand.

How to get there

Take the exit 3 to Torre Chianca from the ring road. Just before Torre Chianca turn left to Torre Rinalda.

GPS coordinates

Latitude: 40.474728 (40° 28' 29.02")
Longitude: 18.173580 (18° 10' 24.8")

Casalabate [Territory map - B-2]

Casalabate is a small fishermen's village, which becomes a popular tourist destination during the summer months. The coastline is predominantly formed by cliffs and coves with crystal clear waters. In common with the other towns and villages along the coast, there is a well preserved 16th century watchtower, called Specchiolla.

How to get there

Take the SS 613 to Brindisi. Just after the town of Squinzano take the SP 96 to Casalabate.

GPS coordinates

Latitude: 40.497315 (40° 29' 50.3")
Longitude: 18.121395 (18° 7' 17.02")

3. La dolce vita

Local cuisine

In common with the rest of Italy, the local cuisine uses many of the ingredients typical of the 'Mediterranean diet', which is now part of the Unesco World Heritage list:

- Seasonal vegetables such as legumes, green beans, cime di rapa (turnip tops), tomatoes, etc.
- Home-made pasta such as orecchiette, trascenate, troccoli and chiancarelle, usually topped with a tomato based sauce, sometimes with meat, fish, or ricotta piccante, another local product.
- Fresh fish and sea-food from the Adriatic.
- Fresh cheeses, the most popular being mozzarella, fresh ricotta, and burrata.
- Extra virgin olive oil, one of the star products of the region which accompanies most dishes, hot or cold.

Typical dishes

Friseddhra

This typical local starter is a bagel-like dry roll that is slightly moistened with water and topped with olive oil, chopped tomatoes, capers and oregano.

Ciceri e tria

Ciceri e tria is a traditional dish said to have originated from the Arabs who once ruled the region. The main ingredients are chickpeas, cooked with onions, tomatoes, parsley, bay leaves and other spices and mixed with fried pasta. It may be served as a starter or main course.

Fave e cicoria

This simple but tasty local dish consists of puréed broad beans accompanied by boiled wild chicory and a drizzle of olive oil. The slightly bitter taste of the wild chicory compliments the sweetish flavour of the broad bean purée.

Fave fritte

This traditional snack consists mainly of broad beans that have been boiled and then fried in abundant olive oil.

Orecchiette alle cime di rapa e mollica

In this variation of the traditional local recipe, orecchiette with turnip tops, fried breadcrumbs anchovies, broccoli and red peppers are added to the pasta for extra flavour.

Orecchiette con salsa di noci

This pasta sauce is prepared by mixing finely chopped walnuts with extra virgin olive oil, salt and pepper to form a creamy paste. This mixture is then used to season the orecchiette.

Ricotta fritta

This recipe consists of thick ricotta slices, breaded and fried in abundant olive oil. This forms a crunchy crust that keeps the ricotta inside soft and creamy.

Scapece

This dish is made with small fried fish that are placed in large wooden tubs, between layers of bread crumbs soaked in vinegar, to which saffron has been added.

Pastries

The region also has its own traditional sweets and pastries, such as cartellate, porceddhruzzi, honey covered pittole and pasticciotti cakes filled with almond paste, jam or cream.

For more Apulian recipes go to www.pugliaandculture.com.

Best restaurants in Lecce

La Torre di Merlino

Great restaurant in the heart of the historical centre, next to piazza Sant'Oronzo. It offers fish and meat specialities. Try the "Burrata in kataifi paste with a mousse made of dried tomatoes and caper flowers", the "Scarbonara", a variant of the famous carbonara and the "Risotto acquerello" with porcini mushrooms and breast of guinea fowl. Excellent selection of beers and a list of over 400 wines.

The restaurant occupies three rooms with high ceilings in an old building. In the summer, they set up tables in the square.

> Via G. B. Del Tufo, 10 [Historic centre map - C-4]
> Telephone: +39 0832 242091

Osteria degli Spiriti

This restaurant offers typical local dishes with a modern twist. They use high quality fresh ingredients and the menu changes seasonally depending on the products available. Tasty pasta, fish and meat dishes as well as delicious home-made desserts.

Closed on Mondays for lunch.

> Via Cesare Battisti, 4 [Historic centre map - D-3]
> Telephone: +39 0832 246274

Le Quattro Spezierie

Le Quattro Spezierie restaurant offers gourmet cuisine with excellent specialities such as "Gallipolini shrimps", "Roasted potatoes with purple cabbage", "Aubergine parmigiana Don Pasta" and "Timballo of pasta and potatoes with podolico cheese of stewed mussels and tomatoes". Excellent desserts with some surprising combinations.

The rooms are modern, elegant and welcoming. In the summer, there is a roof garden with spectacular views of the city and an open-plan food preparation area.

> Via Augusto Imperatore, 19 [Historic centre map - C-4]
> Telephone: +39 0832 246311

La Vecchia Osteria

This simple style restaurant offers traditional cuisine such as handmade orecchiette and various dishes with mussels or seafood. All products are organic and selected with care.

Closed on Monday.

> Via Dasumno, 3 [Historic centre map - B-4]
> Telephone: +39 0832 308057

Vico dei Sotterranei

This restaurant located just behind piazza Duomo offers reasonably priced regional dishes. We suggest you try the "Selection of vegetables with various types of dips and olives", the "Tuna fillet with almonds and oranges", and, for dessert, the traditional pasticciotto leccese.

Closed on Tuesday.

> Vico dei Sotterranei, 3 [Historic centre map - B-4]
> Telephone: +39 320 8368241

Arte dei Sapori

Excellent restaurant in the heart of Lecce with outdoor seating during the summer. Try the "Art of flavours" as a starter, the Tuna steak or the "Pig in Negramaro wine" as a main.

A speciality of this restaurant is the fish baked in clay, where the fish is covered with clay shaped like a fish and then baked in the oven. When ready, the dish is taken to the table and the hardened clay is broken to display the perfectly cooked fish.

Closed on Tuesday.

> Vico degli Alami, 3 [Historic centre map - C-3]
> Telephone: +39 0832 303534

Blu Notte

The cuisine of Blu Notte focuses mainly on fresh fish, which are kept chilled behind a glass window, from which the customers can select their choice. The signature dish is the 'Fresh mint spagoni with diced grouper, clams and cherry tomatoes.

Do not miss the delicious home-made desserts and pastries. Excellent choice of spirits and a wide range of local and national wines.

Closed on Monday and Sunday evening (winter only).

Via Brancaccio Marino, 2 [Historic centre map - C/D-5]
Telephone: +39 0832 304286

Bars & cafés

300mila Lounge Bar

The 300mila Lounge Bar was voted Best Italian Bar in 2013. A great place to have breakfast, a light lunch or some Mediterranean sushi, or just enjoy a drink, a cocktail or one of their excellent wines. Their menus consist mainly of zero-km organic and natural products.

Via 140° Reggimento Fanteria, 11 [Historic centre map - D-4]

Avio Bar

In this bar, situated in the historic centre of the city, Luigi De Mitri makes some of the best coffee around, in all its variations. The "espressino freddo" is a must during the summer months. They also sell a wide range of coffee blends, packaged or loose, coffee liqueurs and jams.

Via Trinchese, 16 [Historic centre map - D-4]

All'Ombra del Barocco

Part of the Liberrima bookshop, the coffee shop All'Ombra del Barocco is situated just outside it. Their outdoor terrace is a great place for a quick lunch, a coffee, or a glass of wine from their excellent selection.

Corte dei Cicala, 9 [Historic centre map - C-4]

La Barrique

La Barrique is a charming café located in the heart of Lecce, a few steps from the Basilica of Santa Croce. A great place to start the day or enjoy a pleasant lunch stop, they use regional products and also do wine tastings.

Via Umberto I, 17 [Historic centre map - C-3]

Mamma Elvira Enoteca

This unpretentious venue in the centre of Lecce does great food, beer and wine. They also offer a selection of cold meats and cheeses to compliment their fine selection of regional wines. On the menu, many home-style dishes like aubergine parmigiana and orecchiette with turnip tops.

Via Umberto I, 19 [Historic centre map - C-3]

Gelaterie & pasticcerie

Pasticceria Natale

Situated next to the Castello Carlo V, this is one of the best pastry shops in Lecce. Apart from excellent ice-cream they make some of the best chocolate around, plus various cakes and pastries typical of the Salento. Not to be missed.

Via Trinchese, 7 [Historic centre map - D-3/4]

Gelateria Martinucci

A long established ice cream parlour, based in the small town of Specchia. Here you can try the traditional Salento ice cream, the spumone. Pistachio and a variety of yoghurt ice creams are some of the other specialities of this gelateria.

Via Giacomo Arditi, 11
[Second road on the left of via Imperatore Adriano - Historic centre map - D-3]

Gelateria di Luca Capilungo

One of the most popular gelaterie among the locals, their specialities include the "pasticciotto leccese" and the "rustico".

Via Bari, 7

Gelateria Sottozero

Not far from Piazza Sant'Oronzo, this small bar does delicious iced coffee, using almond milk syrup, coffee and cream.

Via Giuseppe Giusti, 21
[Third road on the left from via Imperatore Adriano - Historic centre map - D-3]

4. Sport

Golf

Circolo ACAYA Golf & Country SSD ARL

Modern golf centre with driving range, putting green, short game area, bunker, club house, guest house, bar, pool, spa, gym, football pitch and babysitting service.

Masseria San Pietro
Strada provinciale San Cataldo-Otranto, km 5
Acaya – Vernole [Territory Map D-4]
Telephone: +39 0832 861378
Email: info@acayagoldresort.com

GPS coordinates

Latitude: 40.345753 (40° 20' 44.7")
Longitude: 18.311993 (18° 18' 43.1")

Swimming

ICOS

This multi-purpose sports facility has a semi-Olympic swimming pool. The centre is distributed over different levels and has a private car-park.

Via Luigi Einaudi, 12
Telephone: +39 0832 240084
Email: info@icosport.it

GPS coordinates

Latitude: 40.359416 (40° 21' 33.8")
Longitude: 18.158592 (18° 9' 30.9")

MUV

In addition to a gym, there is a 25 meter, 6 lane swimming-pool and a smaller pool, which is used for swimming lessons and water fitness courses.

Via Vittorio Bachelet
Telephone: +39 0832 1816070
Email: info@muvlecce.it

GPS coordinates

Latitude: 40.357077 (40° 21' 25.4")
Longitude: 18.197184 (18° 11 49.8")

Centro Nuoto Lecce

The oldest swimming-pool in Lecce has a family atmosphere and organises swimming lessons and aquatic activities for all ages.

Via Di Ussano, 55 [Historic centre map - B-6]
Telephone: +39 0832 244022

Riding

La Pineta dei Cavalli

Equestrian centre offering horse riding, horse training and a riding school. The riding excursions take place from April to December in the most important places along the coast such as Otranto, Gallipoli and Santa Maria di Leuca. The riding school is open all year round.

Contrada Iacorao, 6
73010 Sogliano Cavour (Le) [Territory map - C-6]
Telephone: +39 328 3176194
Email: info@lapinetadeicavalli.it

GPS coordinates

Latitude: 40.152705 (40° 9' 9.7")
Longitude: 18.211131 (18° 12' 40.07")

Associazione Amici del Murgese

The aim of this place is the promotion of the traditions and culture of the Salento, through the employment of the local breed of Murgese horses. Both horseback riding and riding in antique carriages are available. Courses are organized every day throughout the year on a private or group basis.

Via Fosso Muraglie - trav. Via Torino
73031 Alessano (Le)
Telephone: +39 333 2109278 - +39 339 7576459
Email: info@amicidelmurgese.it

GPS coordinates

Latitude: 39.892100 (39° 53' 31.5")
Longitude: 18.326632 (18° 19' 35.8")

Canoeing

CKCS Kayak Salento

The Canoe Kayak Club Salento is a non-profit sports association founded in 1995. They offer kayaking courses with an emphasis on safe manoeuvering and rescue techniques.

73050 Santa Caterina - Nardò (Le)
Telephone: +39 349 8139599

GPS coordinates

Latitude: 40.139985 (40° 8' 23.9")
Longitude: 17.981851 (17° 58' 54.6")

Skate, surf e winfsurf

Suburban - Surf Skate Windsurf Club

Qualified instructors offer starter Skateboarding, surfing and windsurfing courses. They also organise 'Surfschools' and 'Surfcamps' throughout the year.

Via Zanardelli, 6 - Lecce
Telephone: +39 0832 092372
Email: associazione.suburban@gmail.com

GPS coordinates

Latitude: 40.352433 (40° 21' 8.7")
Longitude: 18.182222 (18° 10' 55.9")

5. Shopping

Crafts

Lecce is also famous for its handmade papier-mâché figures, a long established local craft, whose origins go back to the time of the Counter-Reformation, when, in order to meet an increasing demand for sacred artworks, local artisans resorted to using a combination of paper and other humble materials such as straw, rags, wood and plaster.

La Cartapesta di Claudio Riso

Local craftsman Claudio Riso and his brothers own one of the best papier-mâché shops in Lecce. In their workshop, the Riso brothers create their artworks entirely by hand. There, you can witness the materials being processed and the various objects taking form: from typical local and regional figures to angels and "Pizzica" dancers.

Via Vittorio Emanuele II, 27 [Historic centre map - C-4]
Telephone: +39 0832 243410
Email: info@cartapestariso.it

Artefare

In this store, two papier-mâché artists, Gianno De Carlo and Pinuccia Petruzzelli, sell original objects unlike those traditionally found elsewhere. Many of their unique designs are inspired by nature, such as sea urchins, shells, reeds or leaves.

Via Petronelli, 14 [Historic centre map - C-4]
Telephone: +39 338 228 8416

Cartapesta "Ego" di Marco Galli

Here you can find various types of papier-mâché dolls and objects d'art as well as the more traditional nativity and religious figures.

Piazzetta Castromediano Sigismondo, 9 [Historic centre map - C-3]

Art workshops

In the city centre there are several stonemason's workshops. They continue with the long tradition of carving the same local stone that can be seen on the façades of churches and other monuments. Today, it still inspires the work of many artists who create original and innovative forms.

Laboratorio Tracce

In this workshop you can find unique items made by Ferdinando and Ornella, two artisans trained at the Accademia delle Belle Arti. They create functional works of art such as lamps, vases and bowls.

Corte dei Romiti, 8 [Historic centre map - B-4]

Mi piace by Artefare

Massimiliano De Giovanni has been creating unique home objects such as lamps and vases for years. In collaboration with Ilaria Dell'Onze he has also designed an original line of fashion jewellery items, that combine crystals, gems and stones.

Via Arcivescovo Petronelli, 16 [Historic centre map - C-4]

Markets

Main market

Sunday from 08.00 to 14.00.

Via Umberto I [Historic centre map - C-3]

Antiques market

Every last Sunday of the month from 08.00 to 14.00.

Via XX settembre [Historic centre map - D-5/6]

Organic Food shops

If you are interested in organic food there are some good shops selling interesting locally produced organic food.

Biobottega

Via Benedetto Croce, 45
Telephone: +39 0832 453876

Avio Natura

Via Nicolò Foscarini, 22/24
Telephone: +39 0832 1692894

NaturaSì

Via San Cesario, 153
Telephone: + 39 0832 354201

Wine shops

Nocco Giuseppe

Via Del Palazzo Dei Conti Di Lecce, 27 [Historic centre map -
C-4/5]

Baccus

Via Di Leuca, 85 [Historic centre map - D-6]
Telephone: +39 0832 342256

La casa del primitivo di Manduria

Viale Otranto, 29 [Historic centre map - C/D-5]
Telephone: +39 0832 288651

Linciano Liquors

Duca Degli Abruzzi, 59/61 [Historic centre map - B/C-5]

Striani Ital

Via Benedetto Cairoli [Historic centre map - B-5]
Telephone: +39 0832 301865

Enobar Roll

Via Battisti Cesare, 23 [Historic centre map - D-3]

6. General info

Lecce Wireless City

Lecce Wireless City allows 24 hour free internet access in many areas of the city. To access the service you will need to show some ID and fill out a registration form at one of the following locations:

Comune di Lecce - Sportello E-Gov

Open from 10.00 to 13.00, Monday to Friday and from 15.00 to 17.00, Tuesday and Thursday.

Palazzo Carafa
Entrance via Dei Fedele,1 - first floor [Historic centre map - C-3]
Telephone: +39 0832 682115
Email: leccecittawireless@comune.lecce.it

Comune di Lecce - Ufficio Rel. con il Pubblico

Open from 08.30 to 13.30, Monday to Friday and from 15.30 to 18.00, Tuesday and Thursday.

Palazzo Carafa
Entrance via dei Fedele, 1 [Historic centre map - C-3]
Free phone number: 800 215259

MUST (Museo Storico Città di Lecce)

Open from 10.00 to 13.00 and from 15.00 to 19.00, Tuesday to Sunday.

> Via degli Ammirati, 11 [Historic centre map - C-4]
> Telephone: +39 0832 241067

Presidio Turistico Informativo

Open from 9.00 to 13.30 and from 17.00 to 21.00.

> Via Umberto I, 18 [Historic centre map - C-3]
> Telephone: +39 0832 090523

Banca Popolare Pugliese

> Via XXV Luglio, 31 [Historic centre map - D-3]
> Telephone: +39 0832 247211

Tribunale di Lecce

Open from 7.30 to 14.00, Monday to Friday, from 14.30 to 18.00, Tuesday.

> Viale Michele De Pietro [Historic centre map - C-1/D-2]
> Telephone: +39 0832 660613

Associazione Culturale ACH

Open from 9.00 to 13.00, Monday to Friday.

Via Pettorano, 3
Telephone: +39 328 863 8950

Lido Salapia

Open from 09.00 to 24.00, during summer only.

Via Giovanni Da Verazzano - San Cataldo [Territory map - D-4]
Telephone: +39 0832 650408

Lido York

Open from 08.00 to 20.00, during summer.

Via Amerigo Vespucci, 11 - San Cataldo [Territory map - D-4]
Telephone: +39 340 871 1158

Bikesharing

A bike hiring service is offered at seven locations around the city, where bicycles can be collected and returned from 7.00 to 22.00.

Collection/return points:

Foro Boario [Historic centre map - B-1]
Parcheggio ex Carlo Pranzo [Historic centre map - B-2]
Parcheggio ex arena Aurora [Historic centre map - A-4]
Piazza Santo Oronzo [Historic centre map - C-4]
Piazza Mazzini
Palazzo Alleanza – Via S. Trinchese
Stazione treni [Historic centre map - A-6]

Taxi service

Piazza Santo Oronzo [Historic centre map - C-4]
Telephone: +39 0832 306045

Train station [Historic centre map - A/B-6]
Telephone: +39 0832 247978

Piazza Mazzini
Telephone: +39 0832 246150

Public transports

Trains

Trenitalia

Telephone from abroad: +39 06 684 75475
Telephone from inside Italy: 89 20 21

Ferrovie del Sud-Est

Telephone: +39 0832 315680

Airports

Bari airport

Telephone: +39 080 5800346
aeroportidipuglia.it/bari

Brindisi airport

Telephone: +39 0831 4117208
aeroportidipuglia.it/brindisi

Airport city terminal

Viale Porta Europa [Historic centre map - B-1]
Telephone: +39 0832 256124

Tickets can be bought on the bus or:

- Agenzia Viaggi ELIOS TOURS - Via Salandra, 9
- Agenzia Viaggi MAZZINI - P.zza Mazzini
- Agenzia Theutra (c/o City Terminal)
- Garden Coffee - Via Adriatica, 16
- Boutique Fluxa - Aeroporto Casale

Coaches

Aitolinee Elios

Telephone: +39 0832 871016

Autolinee extraurbane STP

Telephone: +39 0832 228441

Autolinee Urbane SGM

Telephone: +30 0832 230431

Autolinee Sud-Est

Telephone: +39 0832 315680

Salento in Bus

Telephone: +39 345 01001095

Opening hours

Shops

Winter: from 9.00 to 13.00 and from 16.30 to 20.00
Summer: from 9.00 to 13.00 and from 17.00 to 21.00/21.30

All shops open from Monday to Saturday.

Banks

Banks are open Monday to Friday from 8.30 to 13.30. The afternoon time is different from bank to bank. They usually open for about 1 hour from 15.30 to 16.30.

Pharmacies

From 8.00 to 12.30 and from 16.30 to 19.30. On Saturdays and Sundays there is some opening in rota. The ones open are indicated at the entrance of each pharmacy.

Post Offices

The main Post Office in via G. Libertini has the following opening times:

- from 8.00 to 18.30, Monday to Friday
- from 8.00 to 12.30, Saturday

The other Post Offices' opening hours are:

- from 8.00 to 13.30, Monday to Friday
- from 8.00 to 12.30, Saturday

Practicalities

Emergency Numbers

- General emergency number - 112
- Ambulance – 118
- Police – 113
- Fire Fighters – 115

Carabinieri

- Via Lupiae, 6
  Telephone: 112

Cash Dispensers

- Via Vittorio Emanuele II, 15 [Historic centre map - C-4]
- Via Augusto Imperatore, 33 [Historic centre map - C-4]
- Via Sacro Regio Consiglio, 6 [Historic centre map - C-4]
- Piazza Santo Oronzo, 43 [Historic centre map - C-4]
- Via Verdi Giuseppe, 14 [Historic centre map - C-4]
- Piazza S. Oronzo, 15 [Historic centre map - C-4]
- Piazza S. Oronzo, 33 [Historic centre map - C-4]
- Piazza Sant'Oronzo, 39 [Historic centre map - C-4]
- Piazzetta Castromediano Sigismondo, 5 [Historic centre map - C-3]
- Piazzetta G. Riccardi, 9 [Historic centre map - C-3]
- Viale XXV Luglio, 21 [Historic centre map - D-3]
- Viale Lo Re Francesco, 48 [Historic centre map - D-5]
- Viale Quaranta Oronzo, 14 [Historic centre map - B-6]
- Viale Gallipoli, 1 [Historic centre map - B-5]

Cinemas

- Multisala Massimo - Viale Lo Re, 3 [Historic centre map - D-5]
  Telephone: +39 0832 307433
- Cinema Odeon - Via Libertini, 4 [Historic centre map - B-4]
  Telephone: +39 0832 302068
- Teatro Politeama - Via XXV Luglio, 30 [Historic centre map - D-3]
  Telephone: +39 0832 241468
- Cinema S. Lucia - Via S. Lazzaro, 32
  Telephone: +39 0832 343479
- Cinema Antoniano - Via Monte San Michele, 2
  Telephone: +39 0832 392567
- Cinema "DB" dessai - Via Salesiani, 4
  Telephone: +39 0832 390557

- Multisala Medusa - Via Benzi (c/o Ipercoop)
  Telephone: +39 0832 254411

Fire Fighters

- Viale Grazzi, 86
  Telephone: 115

Guardia di Finanza

- Piazzetta Peruzzi, 1
  Telephone: +39 0832 672111

Guardia Medica (Doctor)

- Via Miglietta, 15
  Telephone: +39 0832 343460 / +39 0832 215811

Hospital

- P.F. Muratore
  Telephone: +39 0832 661111

Parking-lots

- Foro Boario - Viale Adua [Historic centre map - B-3]
- Carlo Pranzo - Via Vito Carluccio [Historic centre map - A-1]
- Via F. Calasso [Historic centre map - C-1]

Pharmacies

- Dr.ssa Conte - Via F. Rubichi, 41

- Dr. De Carlo - Via di Vaste, 68 [Historic centre map - A-3]
- Dr. De Pascalis - Via Birago Dalmazio, 11
- Dr Bianco Curto - Piazzetta Argento Nicodemo, 4 [Historic centre map - C-6]
- Casciaro - Via Gentile Giovanni, 20
- Dr.essa De Marco - Via delle Rose
- Dr.ssa De Marco - Piazza Alberti, 6
- Dr.ssa De Marco - Via Marco Polo, 6
- Dr De Marco - Via Trinchese , 22 [Historic centre map - D-3/4]
- De Pace Licignano - Via Oberdan, 26
- Degli Atti - Via Leuca, 11
- Farmacia Del Cigno - Via Vittorio Emanuele II, 66 [Historic centre map - C-4]
- Del Popolo Lolli - Viale Repubblica, 84
- Dr Guarrera - Via Lecce, 109
- Dr Giubba - Piazza Napoli, 8
- Elia - Via Di Leuca, 115
- Ferocino - Piazza Sant'Oronzo, 31 [Historic centre map - C-4]
- Galizia - Via Taranto 29 [Historic centre map - A/B-2]
- Guglielmi - Piazza Sant'Oronzo, 18 [Historic centre map - C-4]
- Marzano - Via del Mare, 6A

Police

- Viale Otranto, 1 [Historic centre map - D-5]
  Telephone: +39 0832 453411

Post Offices

Main Post-office

- Piazza Libertini, 5/6 [Historic centre map - D-4]

Telephone: +39 0832 274069

Other post offices

- Piazzale Stazione [Historic centre map - A/B-6]
  Telephone: 0832 244491
- Viale Cavallotti Felice 1 [Historic centre map - D-3/4]
  Telephone: +39 0832 274111
- Viale Marche, 21/C [Historic centre map - C-6]
  Telephone: +39 0832 236449, 0832 347776
- Via Taranto, 58 [Historic centre map - A/B-2]
  Telephone: +39 0832 242423
- Via Principi Di Savoia, 4 [Historic centre map - C-3]
  Telephone: +39 0832 242079

Provincial Council (Provincia)

- Via Umberto I, 13 [Historic centre map - C-3]
  Telephone: +39 0832 6831

Regione Puglia (Puglia region)

- Viale Aldo Moro
  Telephone: +39 0832 373111

Street Wardens

- Viale Rossini, 110
  Telephone: +39 0832 233211

Tourist Information offices

- Corso Vittorio Emanuele II, 24 [Historic centre map - C-4]
  Telephone: +39 0832 682985
- Castello Carlo V, viale XXV Luglio [Historic centre map - D-4]
  Telephone: +39 0832 246517
- Sedile Comunale, Piazza Sant'Oronzo [Historic centre map - C-4]
  Telephone: +39 0832 242099
- Email: info.lecce@viaggiareinpuglia.it

Town Hall (Comune)

- Palazzo Carafa - Via Rubichi [Historic centre map - C-3]
  Telephone: +39 0831 307000

7. Day trips

Otranto

Otranto, situated on the Adriatic coast of Salento peninsula, is an ancient town that recently became part of the World Heritage as a Site Messenger of Peace. It also is a member of the club "The most beautiful villages in Italy". Of great interest is the Cathedral of the Annunciation with a beautiful mosaic, made between 1163 and 1165 by the monk Pantaleon.

Tourist info office

Piazza Castello
Telephone: +39 0836 801436

How to get there

By car

Otranto can be reached by taking the SS16 Adriatica, exit 11B from the ring road of Lecce.

Ditance: 47 km
Journey time: about 40 minutes

By train

Lecce is connected to Otranto by the Ferrovie del Sud-Est departing from Lecce train station. Journey time: about 1 hour 30 minutes

GPS coordinates

Latitude: 40.144486 (40° 8' 40")
Longitude: 18.492393 (18° 29' 32")

[Map of places of interest in Puglia - F-4]

Gallipoli

Gallipoli is located along the west coast of the Salento peninsula, jutting out into the Ionian Sea and divided into two parts: the village on the mainland and the old town on a small island. There are here interesting buildings and religious architecture of the Baroque period such as the Cathedral, the church of St. Agatha and the church of San Francesco di Paola. Also the Greek fountain built around the third century BC, believed to be the oldest fountain in Italy.

Tourist info office

Piazza Imbriani, 10
Telephone: +39 0833 262529

How to get there

By car

Gallipoli can easily be reached by taking the SS 101 that leads directly to the city. To get to the SS 101 take exit 13B from the Lecce ring road.

Distance: 42 km
Journey time: about 35 minutes

By train

Gallipoli is connected with Lecce by the Ferrovie del Sud-Est departing from Lecce train station.
Journey time: about 1 hour and 20 minutes

GPS coordinates

Latitude: 40.055944 (40° 43' 55")
Longitude: 17.978610 (17° 33' 41")

[Map of places of interest in Puglia - F-4]

Ostuni

Ostuni is the most typical and most representative town of Puglia. Its beautiful white historic centre located on a hill is surrounded by a defensive wall built originally by the Messapi and then redesigned by the Aragonese. Ostuni has also a gorgeous surrounding area dominated by green olive trees that stretch down to a long coast scattered with lovely beaches.

Tourist info office

Corso Mazzini, 6
Telephone: +39 0831 301268

How to get there

By car

Head north towards Brindisi and Bari. Take the SS 613 and then the SS 379 (E55). After about 65 km take the exit 'Torre Pozzella-Ostuni' and follow signs to Ostuni.

Distance: 77 km
Journey time: about 1 hour

By train

Ostuni is well connected by the National Railways (Trenitalia) departing from Lecce train station. Ostuni Station is 2 km from the city, therefore, to get to the city centre you will need to use public transport or take a taxi.
Journey time: about 1 hour

GPS coordinates

Latitude: 40.732088 (40° 3' 21")
Longitude: 17.578242 (17° 58' 42")

[Map of places of interest in Puglia - E-3]

Alberobello

Alberobello is a town famous for its special cone-shaped houses called trulli, today part of the UNESCO World Heritage. The main areas of the city, Monti and Aia Piccola are entirely built of trulli perched on the hills. A stunning setting that never fails to enchant and that must be seen.

Tourist info office

Via Monte Nero, 3
Telephone +39 080 432 2060

How to get there

By car

You can reach the city by taking the SS 613 towards Brindisi, then the SS 379 direction Bari. At about 93 km from Lecce take the exit direction Fasano. From here take the SS 172dir, then the SP1 and the SP 81, following signs to Alberobello.

Distance: 114 km
Journey time: about 1 hour and 20 minutes

By train

Lecce is connected to Alberobello by the Ferrovie del Sud-Est departing form the Lecce train station. Journey time: about 2 hours

GPS coordinates

Latitude: 40.782231 (40° 46' 56")
Longitude: 17.237656 (17° 14' 15")

[Map of places of interest in Puglia - D-3]

Grotte di Castellana

The caves of Castellana are located near the town of Castellana Grotte. These are Italy's most famous caves and one of the main attractions of Puglia. It is possible to visit several caves, each with its own name such as the Grotta Nera (Black Cave), the Cavernone dei Monumenti (Monuments Cave), the Grotta della Civetta (Owl Cave) and the most wonderful one the Grotta Bianca (White Cave).

Information

Piazzale Anelli, Castellana Grotte
Telephone: +39 080 4998221

How to get there

By car

Take the SS 613 towards Brindisi and then continue on the SS 379 towards Bari. At about 105 km from Lecce take the exit "Castellana Grotte" and continue on the SP 237 direction Grotte di Castellana.

Distance: 123 km
Journey time: about 1 hour and 20 minutes

By train

To reach Castellana Caves take a Ferrovie del Sud-Est train from Lecce station. Journey time: about 3 hours and 30 minutes

GPS coordinates

Latitude: 40.875890 (40° 52' 33")
Longitude: 17.148392 (17° 8' 54")

[Map of places of interest in Puglia - D-3]

Castel del Monte

Castel del Monte is one of the symbols of Puglia and one of the most famous monuments of the times of Frederick II. It was built in the first half of the thirteenth century on a hill of the Apulian Murgia, near the city of Andria.

Information

Telephone: +39 0883 592 283

How to get there

By car

Castel del Monte can only be reached by car. Take the SS 379 to Bari and then continue towards Modugno, Bitonto and Ruvo di Puglia using the SP 231.

Distance: 205 km
Journey time: about 2 hours and 20 minutes.

GPS coordinates

Latitude: 41.084538 (41° 5' 4")
Longitude: 16.270087 (16° 16' 12")

[Map of places of interest in Puglia - C-2]

Martina Franca

Martina Franca, located on a high slope of the Murgia hills called Monte San Martino, is a city famous for its Baroque buildings such as the palaces Panelli, Blasi and Motolese, for the splendid Basilica of San Martino, and for other churches in the Baroque style scattered inside its characteristic old town. The city is also famous for the lyric/classical music festival of the Valle d'Itria, usually held in late July.

Tourist info office

Piazza XX Settembre, 3
Telephone: +39 080 480 5702

How to get there

By car

Take the SS 613 and then the SS 379 (E55) towards Brindisi-Bari. At about 64 km from Lecce take the exit 'Torre Pozzella-Ostuni' and follow signs to Ostuni. Once in Ostuni take the ring road and follow signs for Martina Franca (SP 14).

Distance: 102 km
Journey time: about 1 hour and 20 minutes

By train

Lecce is connected to Martina Franca by the Ferrovie del Sud-Est departing from Lecce train station. Journey time: about 1 hour and 40 minutes

GPS coordinates

Latitude: 40.705522 (40° 42' 19")
Longitude: 17.336511 (17° 20' 11")

[Map of places of interest in Puglia - D-3]

8. Historic centre map

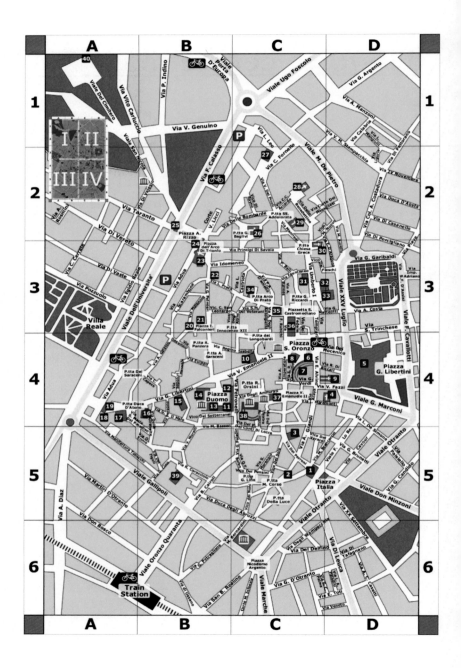

Places on map

1	Porta San Biagio	21	Palazzo Palmieri
2	Chiesa Madre di Dio	22	Teatro Paisiello
3	Chiesa di San Matteo	23	Chiesa di Santa M. della Porta
4	Chiesa di San Giuseppe	24	Porta Napoli
5	Castello di Carlo V	25	Obelisco
6	Colonna di Santo Oronzo	26	Chiesa delle Alcantarine
7	Anfiteatro Romano	27	Chiesa di S. M. degli Angeli
8	Palazzo del Sedile	28	Chiesa di S.G. Evangelista
9	Chiesa di Santa M. delle Grazie	29	Chiesa di Sant'Angelo
10	Chiesa di Santa Irene	30	Chiesa Greca
11	Duomo	31	Palazzo Adorno
12	Campanile	32	Convento dei Celestini
13	Palazzo Vescovile	33	Basilica di Santa Croce
14	Palazzo del Seminario	34	Arco di Prato
15	Chiesa di Santa Teresa	35	Chiesa del Gesù
16	Chiesa di Sant'Anna ed il C.	36	Palazzo Carafa
17	Chiesa di S.G. Battista al Rosario	37	Chiesa di Santa Chiara
18	Convento dei Domenicani	38	Teatro Romano
19	Porta Rudiae	39	Chiesa del Carmine
20	Palazzo Marrese	40	Chiesa dei S.S. N. e Cataldo

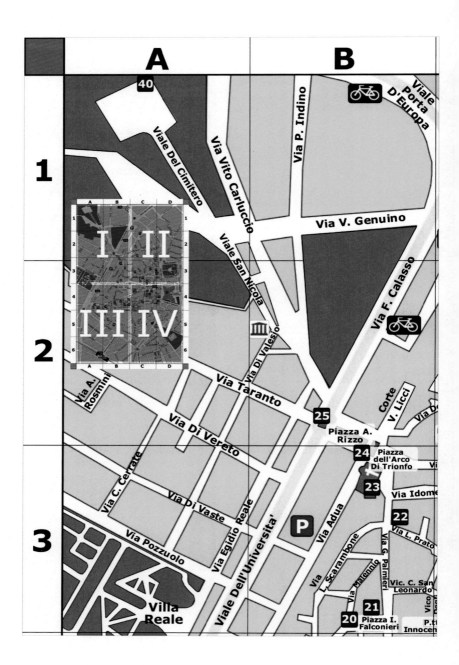

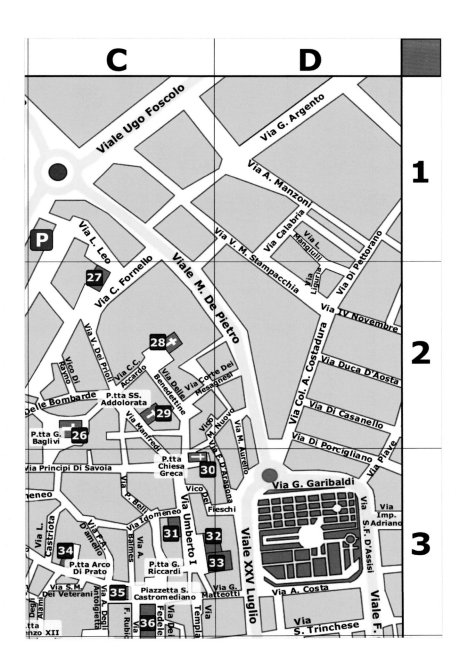

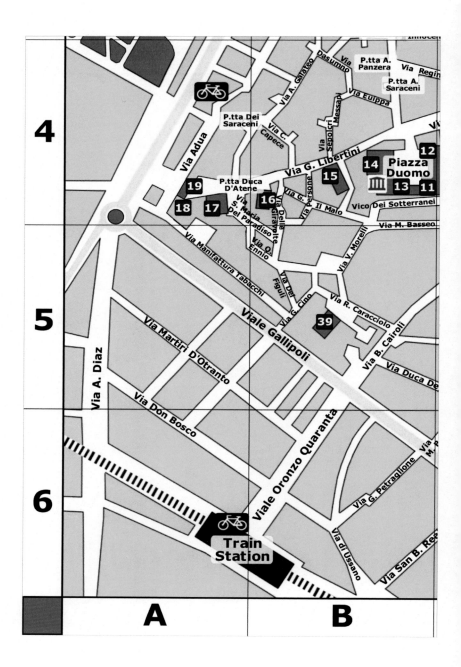

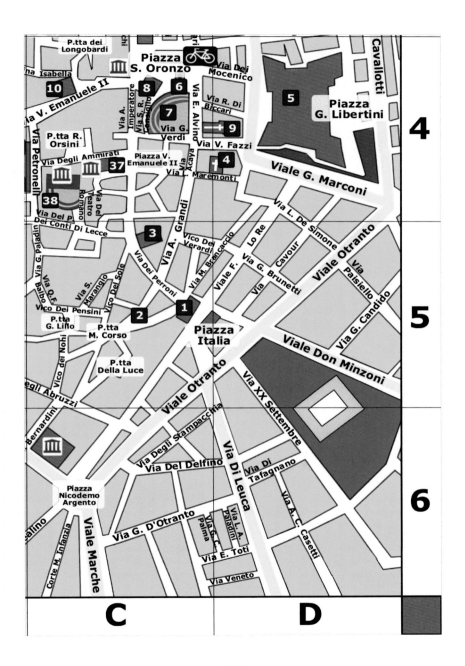

P.tta dei Longobardi

na Isabella

Piazza S. Oronzo

Via Dei Mocenico

10

Via V. Emanuele II

8

6

Via R. Di Biccari

5

Piazza G. Libertini

Cavallotti

4

Via A. Imperatore

Via S. R.

7

Via E. Alvino

Via G. Verdi

9

Via V. Fazzi

P.tta R. Orsini

Via Petronelli

Via Degli Ammirati

37

Piazza V. Emanuele II

Via L. Maremonti

4

Viale G. Marconi

Via Del Teatro Romano

38

Via Del P.

Dei Conti Di Lecce

Via L. De Simone

3

Via A. Grandi

Vico Dei Verardi

Via M. Brancaccio

Lo Re

Via G. Brunetti

Cavour

Via L. De Simone

Viale Otranto

Via Paisiello

Via G.Paladini

Via Q.F. Balbo

Via S. Marangio

Vico Del Sole

Via Dei Perroni

Via F.

Via G. Candido

Vico Dei Pensini

P.tta G. Lillo

P.tta M. Corso

2

1

Piazza Italia

Viale Don Minzoni

5

P.tta Della Luce

Vico dei Nohi

egli Abruzzi

Viale Otranto

Via XX Settembre

Bernardini

Via Degli Stampacchia

Via Del Delfino

Via Di Leuca

Via Di Tafagnano

Piazza Nicodemo Argento

calino

Corte M. Infanzia

Viale Marche

Via G. D'Otranto

Via G. C. Palma

Via L.A. Paladini

Via A. C. Casetti

6

Via E. Toti

Via Veneto

C

D

Addresses on map

Acaya, via	**C-4**	Don Bosco, via	**A-5/6**
Accardo Corte Conte, via	**C-2**	Don Minzoni, viale	**D-5**
Addolorata S.S., piazzetta	**C-2**	Duca D'Aosta, via	**D-2**
Adriano Imperatore, via	**D-3**	Duca D'Atene, piazzetta	**A/B-4**
Adua, via	**B-3/4**	Duca Degli Abruzzi, via	**B/C-5**
Alvino Ernesto, via	**C-4**	Duomo, piazza	**B-4**
Arco Di Prato, via	**C-3**	Egidio Reale, via	**A-3**
Argento Gaetano, via	**D-1**	Ennio Quinto, via	**A-5**
Augusto Imperatore, via	**C-4**	Euippa, via	**B-4**
Aurelio Marco, via	**D-2/3**	Falconieri Ignazio, piazza	**B-3**
Baglivi Giorgio, piazzetta	**C-2**	Fanteria 140 RGT, via	**D-4**
Balbo Quinto Fabio, via	**C-5**	Fazzi Vito, via	**D-4**
Balmes Abramo, via	**C-3**	Fornello Casale, via	**C-2**
Basseo Marco, via	**B-4**	Galateo Antonio, via	**B-4**
Battisti Cesare, via	**D-3**	Gallipoli, viale	**B-5**
Belli Pietro, via	**C-3**	Garibaldi Giuseppe, via	**D-3**
Bernardini Mario, via	**C-6**	Genuino Vespasiano, via	**B-1**
Brancaccio Marino, via	**C/D-5**	Grandi Ascanio, via	**C-4/5**
Brunetti Gaetano, via	**D-5**	Idomeneo, via	**B/C-3**
Cairoli Benedetto, via	**B-5**	Il Malo Guglielmo, via	**B-4**
Calabria, via	**D-1**	Indino Pietro, via	**B-1**
Calasso Francesco, via	**B-2**	Innocenzo XII, piazzetta	**B-3**
Candido Giuseppe, via	**D-5**	Italia, piazza	**D-5**

Capece Corrado, via	**B-4**	IV Novembre, via	**D-2**
Caracciolo Roberto, via	**B-5**	Leo Leonardo, via	**C-1**
Carluccio Vito, via	**A-1**	Libertini G., piazza	**D-4**
Casetti Antonio C., via	**D-6**	Libertini Giuseppe, via	**B-4**
Castriota Isabella, via	**C-3**	Licci Vincenzo, corte	**B-2**
Castromediano S., p.tta	**C-3**	Liguria, via	**D-2**
Cavallotti Felice, viale	**D-3/4**	Lillo Giuseppe, piazzetta	**C-5**
Cavour, via	**D-5**	Lo Re Francesco, via	**D-5**
Cerrate Casale, via	**A-3**	Malennio, via	**B-3**
Chiesa Greca, piazzetta	**C-3**	Manfredi, via	**C-2**
Cino Giuseppe, via	**B-5**	Mangiulli Luigi, via	**D-1**
Consiglio Sacro Regio, via	**C-4**	Manifattura Tabacchi, via	**A-5**
Corso Mariotto, piazzetta	**C-5**	Manzoni Alessandro, via	**D-1**
Corte dei Mesagnesi, via	**C-2**	Marangio Sindaco, via	**C-5**
Costa Achille, via	**D-3**	Marche, viale	**C-6**
Costadura Col. A., via	**D-2**	Marconi Guglielmo, via	**D-4**
D'Amelio F. A., via	**C-3**	Maremonti Ludovico, via	**C/D-4**
D'Aragona Federico, via	**D-3**	Martiri D'Otranto, via	**A-5**
D'Otranto G., via	**C-6**	Matteotti Giacomo, via	**D-3**
Dasumno, via	**B-4**	Morelli Vincenzo, via	**B-5**
De Pietro M., via	**C-1**	Nicodemo A., piazza	**C-6**
De Simone Luigi, via	**D-5**	Nuovo Mondo, vico	**C/D-2**
De Tufo G.B., via	**C-4**	Oronzo Quaranta, via	**B-6**
Degli Alami, via	**C-3**	Orsini R., piazzetta	**C-4**
Degli Ammirati, via	**C-4**	Otranto, viale	**D-5**
Degli Antoglietta, via	**C-3**	Paisiello, via	**D-5**

Degli Stampacchia, via	**C-6**	Paladini Guglielmo, via	**C-5**
Dei Cicala, corte	**C4**	Paladini Luisa A., via	**D-6**
Dei Fedele, via	**C-3**	Palma G. C., via	**C/D-6**
Dei Fieschi, via	**C/D-3**	Palmieri Giuseppe, via	**B-3**
Dei Figuli, via	**B-5**	Panzera A., piazzetta	**B-4**
Dei Longobardi, piazzetta	**C-4**	Personé Ermenegildo, via	**B-4**
Dei Mocenico, via	**D-4**	Petraglione Giuseppe, via	**B-6**
Dei Nohi, vico	**C-5**	Petronelli, via	**C-4**
Dei Pensini, vico	**C-5**	Piave, via	**D-3**
Dei Perroni, via	**C-5**	Porta D'Europa, viale	**B-1**
Dei Prioli V., via	**C-2**	Pozzuolo, via	**A-3**
Dei Romiti, corte	**B-4**	Prato Leonardo, via	**B-3**
Dei Saraceni, piazzetta	**A-4**	Principi Di Savoia, via	**C-3**
Dei Sotterranei, via	**B-4**	Regina Isabella, via	**B/C-4**
Dei Verardi, vico	**C-5**	Riccardi G., piazzetta	**C-3**
Dei Veterani S.M., via	**C-3**	Rizzo Angelo, piazza	**B-2**
Del Cimitero, viale	**A-1**	Rosmini Antonio, via	**A-2**
Del Delfino, via	**C-6**	Rubichi Francesco, via	**C-3**
Del Palazzo dei Conti Di Lecce, via	**C-5**	San Bernardino Realino, via	**B/C-6**
Del Sole, vico	**C-5**	San Fran. D'Assisi, via	**D-3**
Del Teatro Romano, via	**C-4**	San Leonardo Conservatorio, vicolo	**B-3**
Dell'arco Di Trionfo, piazza	**B-3**	San Nicola, viale	**A-1/B-2**
Dell'Università, viale	**A-3**	Santa Maria dei V., via	**C-3**

Della Corte Dei Mesagnesi, via	C/D-2	Santa Maria del P., via	A-4
Della Luce, piazzetta	C-5	Santo Oronzo, piazza	C-4
Delle Benedettine, via	C-2	Scarambone Luigi, via	B-3
Delle Bombarde, via	C-2	Sepolcri Messapi, via	B-4
Delle Giravolte, via	B-4	Stampacchia V. M., via	D-1/2
Di Biccari Roberto, via	D-4	Taranto, via	A/B-2
Di Casanello, via	D-2	Templari, via	C-3
Di Leuca, via	D-6	Toti Enrico, via	C/D-6
Di Pettorano, via	D-1/2	Trinchese Salvatore, via	D-3/4
Di Porcigliano, via	D-2/3	Ugo Foscolo, via	C-1
Di Rayno, via	C-2	Umberto I, via	C-3
Di Tafagnano, via	D-6	Veneto, via	D-6
Di Ussano, via	B-6	Vereto, via	A-2
Di Valesio, via	B-2	Vittorio E. II, piazza	C-4
Di Vaste, via	A-3	Vittorio Emanuele II, via	C-4
Di Vereto, via	A-2	XX Settembre, via	D-5/6
Diaz Armando, via	A-5	XXV Luglio, viale	D-3

9. Territory map

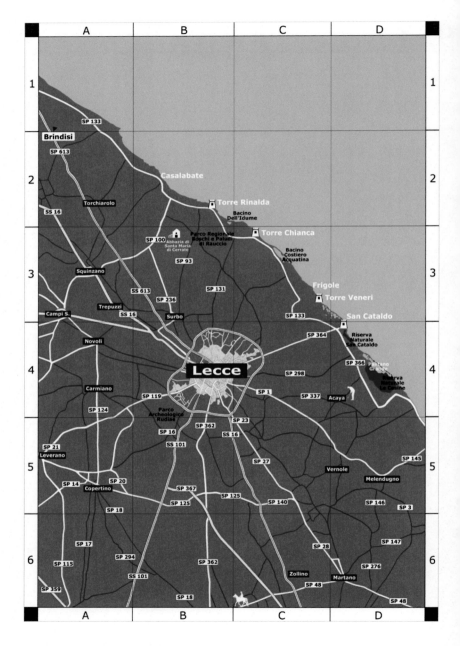

Places on map

Abbazia di Santa Maria di Cerrate	**B-3**		Parco Archeologico Rudiae	**B-4**
Acaya	**D-4**		Parco regionale Boschi e Paludi di Rauccio	**B-3**
Bacino Costiero Acquatina	**C-3**		Riserva naturale Le Cesine	**D-4**
Bacino dell'Idume	**B-2**		Riserva naturale San Cataldo	**D-4**
Campi Salentina	**A-3**		San Cataldo	**D-3**
Carmiano	**A-4**		Squinzano	**A-3**
Casalabate	**B-2**		Surbo	**B-3**
Copertino	**A-5**		Torchiarolo	**A-2**
Frigole	**C-3**		Torre Chianca	**C-3**
Lecce	**B-4**		Torre Rinalda	**B-2**
Leverano	**A-5**		Torre Veneri	**C-3**
Martano	**D-6**		Trepuzzi	**A-3**
Melendugno	**D-5**		Vernole	**D-5**
Novoli	**A-4**		Zollino	**C-6**
Pantano Grande	**D-4**			

10. Railways map of Puglia

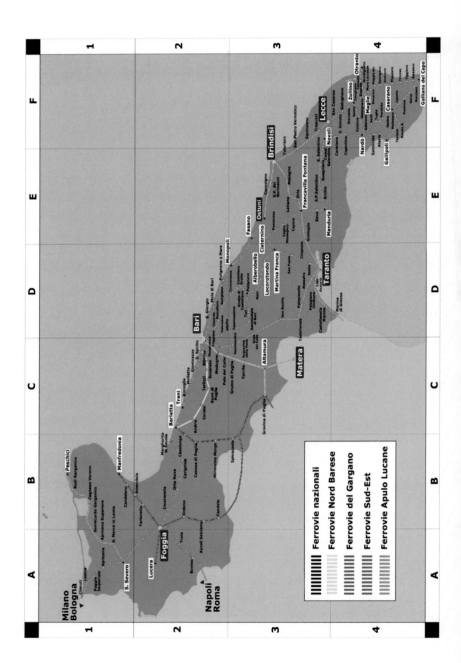

Ferrovie nazionali
Ferrovie Nord Barese
Ferrovie del Gargano
Ferrovie Sud–Est
Ferrovie Apulo Lucane

130

F N = Ferrovie Nazionali
F SE = Ferrovie Sud-Est
F AL = Ferrovie Apulo Lucane
F NB = Ferrovie Nord Barese
F DG = Ferrovie del Gargano

Acquaviva delle Fonti	F N	C3		Mesagne	F N	E3
Adelfia	F SE	D2		Miggiano	F SE	F4
Alberobello	F SE	D3		Minervino Murge	F N	B2
Alessano	F SE	F4		Modugno	F AL	C2
Alezio	F SE	F4		Mola di Bari	F N	D2
Altamura	F AL	C3		Molfetta	F N	C2
Amendola	F N	B2		Monopoli	F N	D3
Andrano	F SE	F4		Morciano	F SE	F4
Andria	F NB	C2		Mungivacca	F SE	D2
Apricena	F N	A1		Muro Leccese	F SE	F4
Apricena Superiore	F DG	A1		Nardò	F SE	F4
Ascoli Satriano	F N	B2		Noci	F SE	D3
Bagnolo	F SE	F4		Noicattaro	F SE	D2
Bari	FN/F SE/F AL	D2		Novoli	F SE	F3
Barletta	F N	C2		Ordona	F N	B2
Bisceglie	F N	C2		Oria	F N	E3
Bitonto	F NB	C2		Orta Nova	F N	B2
Bovino	F N	A2		Ostuni	F N	E3

Brindisi	F N	E3	Otranto	F SE	F4
Cagnano Varano	F DG	B1	Palagianello	F N	D3
Campi Salentina	F SE	E3	Palagiano Chiatone	F N	D3
Candela	F N	B2	Palo del Colle	F AL	C2
Candelaro	F N	B1	Parabita	FSE	F4
Cannole	F SE	F4	Pascarosa	F SE	E3
Canosa di Puglia	F N	B2	Peschici	F DG	B1
Capece	F SE	E3	Poggiardo	F SE	F4
Capurso	F SE	D2	Poggio Imperiale	F N	A1
Carmiano	F SE	F4	Polignano a Mare	F N	D2
Carovigno	F N	E3	Presicce	F SE	F4
Casalonga	F N	B2	Putignano	F SE	D3
Casamassima	F SE	D3	Racale A.	F SE	F4
Casarano	F SE	F4	Rodi Garganico	F DG	B1
Castellana Grotte	F SE	D3	Rutigliano	F SE	D2
Castellaneta	FN	D3	Ruvo di Puglia	F NB	C2
Castellaneta Marina	FN	D3	S. Salentino	F SE	E3
Ceglie Messapica	F SE	E3	S.P. Salentino	F SE	E3
Cerignola	F N	B2	Salve	F SE	F4
Chieuti	F N	A1	Sammichele di Bari	F SE	D3
Cisternino	F N/F SE	E3	San Basilio	F N	D3
Conversano	F SE	D3	San Cesareo	F SE	F4
Copertino	F SE	F4	San Donato	F SE	F4
Corato	F NB	C2	San Giorgio	F N	D2

Corigliano	F SE	**F4**	San Marco in Lamis	**F DG**	**A1**
Crispiano	F SE	**D3**	San Paolo	F SE	**D3**
Erchie	F SE	**E3**	San Pietro Vernotico	**F N**	**E3**
Fasano	F N	**E3**	San Severo	**F N**	**A1**
Foggia	F N	**B2**	San vito dei Normanni	**F N**	**E3**
Francavilla Fontana	F N/F SE	**E3**	Sanarica	F SE	**F4**
Galatina	F SE	**F4**	Sanicardo Garganico	**F DG**	**A1**
Galatone	F SE	**F4**	Sanicola	F SE	**F4**
Galliano del Capo	F SE	**F4**	Sannicandro	**F N**	**C3**
Gallipoli	F SE	**F4**	Santo Spirito	**F N**	**C2**
Galugnano	F SE	**F4**	Sava	F SE	**E3**
Gioia del Colle	F N	**D3**	Secli	F SE	**F4**
Giovinazzo	F N	**C2**	Soleto	F SE	**F4**
Giurdignao	F SE	**F4**	Sovereto	**F NB**	**C2**
Gravina di Puglia	FN/F AL	**C3**	Spinazzola	**F N**	**B3**
Grottaglie	F N	**E3**	Spongano	F FS	**F4**
Grotte di Castellana	F SE	**D3**	Squinzano	**F N**	**F3**
Grumo di Puglia	F AL	**C3**	Statte	F SE	**D3**
Guagnano	F SE	**E3**	Sternatia	F SE	**F4**
Incoronata	F N	**B2**	Taranto	FN/F SE	**D3**
Latiano	F N	**E3**	Taviano	F SE	**F4**
Lecce	FN/F	**F3**	Terlizzi	**F NB**	**C2**

	SE				
Lesina	F N	**A1**	Tiggiano	F SE	**F4**
Lido Azzurro	F N	**D3**	Torrito	F AL	**C3**
Locorotondo	F SE	**D3**	Tortorella	F N	**B2**
Lucera	F N	**A2**	Trani	F N	**C2**
Maglie	F SE	**F4**	Trepuzzi	F N	**F3**
Manduria	F SE	**E3**	Tricase	F SE	**F4**
Manfredonia	F N	**B1**	Triggiano	F SE	**D2**
Margherita di Savoia	F N	**B2**	Troia	F N	**A2**
Marina di Ginosa	F N	**D4**	Tuglie	F SE	**F4**
Martina Franca	F SE	**D3**	Turi	F SE	**D3**
Massafra	F N	**D3**	Tuturano	F N	**E3**
Matera	F AL	**C3**	Ugento	F SE	**F4**
Matino	F SE	**F4**	Valenzano	F SE	**D2**
Melissano	F SE	**F4**	Zollino	F SE	**F4**
Melpignano	F SE	**F4**			

11. Map of places of interest in Puglia

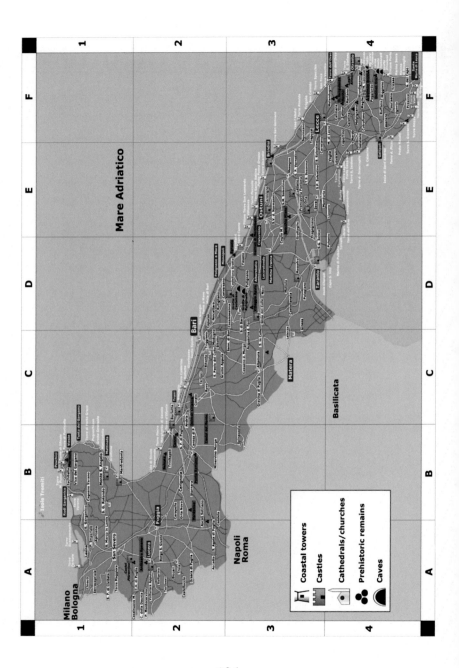

Places on map

Alberobello	**D3**		Manfredonia	**B1**
Altamura	**C3**		Martina Franca	**D3**
Andria	**C2**		Massafra	**D3**
Ascoli Satriano	**A2**		Matera	**C3**
Bari	**C2**		Mattinata	**B1**
Bitonto	**C2**		Mattinatella	**B1**
Brindisi	**E3**		Melendugno	**F4**
Canne	**B2**		Melpignano	**F4**
Canosa di Puglia	**B2**		Merinum	**B1**
Castel del Monte	**C2**		Mesagne	**E3**
Castel Fiorentino	**A1**		Molfetta	**C2**
Ceglie Messapica	**E3**		Monopoli	**D2**
Cerignola	**B2**		Monte Sant'Angelo	**B1**
Cisternino	**D3**		Oria	**E3**
Conversano	**D2**		Ostuni	**E3**
Dolmen Chianca	**C2**		Otranto	**F4**
Dolmen di Montalbano	**E3**		Peschici	**B1**
Dolmen Oru	**F4**		Poligano a Mare	**D2**
Dolmen Scusi	**F4**		Ponte Romano	**B2**
Eganzia	**D3**		Porto Cesareo	**E4**
Fasano	**D3**		Pugnochiuso	**B1**
Foggia	**A2**		Punta Prosciutto	**E4**
Gallipoli	**F4**		Rodi Garganico	**B1**
Gioia del Colle	**D3**		S.G. Rotondo	**B1**

Giurdignano	F4	San Marco in Lamis	A1
Grotta dei Cervi	F4	San Severo	A1
Grotta di Putignano	D3	Santa Maria di Leuca	F4
Grotta Smeralda	B1	Selapia	B2
Grotta Zinzulusa	F4	Taranto	D3
Grottaglie	E3	Testa del Gargano	B1
Grotte di Castellana	D3	Torre dell'Orso	F4
Herdoniae	B2	Torre dell'Ovo	E4
Isole Tremiti	B1	Torre Guaceto	E3
Laghi Alimini	F4	Torre S. Giovanni	F4
Latiano	E3	Trani	C2
Lecce	F3	Troia	A2
Locorotondo	D3	Vieste	B1
Lucera	A2	Volturino	A2
Manduria	E3	Zollino	F4

Publisher

www.pugliaandculture.com

Author

Francesco Flore

Editor

Ignacio Ruiz-Laorden

Made in the USA
San Bernardino, CA
19 September 2016